I0439098

Living the Personal Myth:

Making the Magic of Faerie
Real in One's Own Life

By The Silver Elves

Copyright © 2014 The Silver Elves, Michael J Love and Martha C. Love

All rights reserved.

ISBN-13: 978-1497550391

ISBN-10: 1497550394

Printed in the United States of America by CreateSpace

Without limiting the rights under the copyright reserved above, no part of this publication may be reproduced, stored in or introduced into a retrieval system, or transmitted in any form or by any means (electronic, mechanical, by photocopying, recording or otherwise) without the prior written permission of the copyright owner and the publisher of the book.

DEDICATION

This book is dedicated to Oberon and Morning Glory for always having the courage to dress up and come out to play. You are an inspiration to us all.

Some people say,
"Fake It Till you Make It"
but we elves say,
"Be It Until You Become It".
—The Silver Elves

TABLE OF CONTENTS

CHAPTER 3:

THE DEVELOPMENT OF MY PERSONAL MYTH.... 53

CHAPTER 4:

CHAPTER 5:

METHODS 103

CHAPTER 6:

ENTERING ELFIN: AN INTEGRATED IMAGINAL PROCESS..115

CHAPTER 7:

CHAPTER 8:

Most people are afraid
and avoid the homeless
and the street people
and look down on them.
But we elves know many of them
to be our very own faerie folk
just so damaged by the world
that they cannot find
an easy place within it.

INTRODUCTION:

"GIVE ME THE GLORY OF FAËRIE TILL I TIRE OF ALL THE IMAGES."

(WAITE, 1974, P. 165)

This book began as: *A Depth Inquiry into the use of the personal myth as a process for exploring the magical world of the unconscious* as a thesis submitted to Sonoma State University in partial fulfillment of the requirements for the degree of Master of Arts in Psychology. This was Zardoa's second Master's Degree, the first being a Master of Science in Communications from Southern Illinois University in Carbondale where he first encountered the Elf Queen's Daughters and shortly thereafter established the Elves of the Southern Woodlands vortex of that Sisterhood, which evolved into the Sylvyn Elves in Gainesville, Fl. and the Silver Elves when we moved to California (see our books the *Magical Elven Love Letters, vols. 1, 2 & 3.*)

Because of the limitations of an academic thesis we have edited that work removing those elements that we thought would be uninteresting to our readers (but were necessary for a Thesis) and expanding it to include those things and ideas that were beyond the scope of a strictly psychological study.

After presenting his thesis, one of his advisors commented that she had always thought he was joking when he said he was an elf but now that she had read the thesis she could see that he really meant it. In part this was true because in order to move effortlessly through the academic world as well as the frequently judgmental world of normal folk, these elves often test the waters, so to speak, by revealing our true identities with a tone that one could assume, if that is their inclination, that we are just teasing them, or being playful when we disclose we are elves. In this way we can gauge the individual's reaction and reveal more of our elven natures if we deem it appropriate and safe. Like many elf, faerie, otherkin, we are sensitive to the fact that most people do not believe we exist and tend to ridicule those who assume a different personae than those approved by the dominant culture of their society. When we tell people, quite lightly, that we are elfin they tend to either laugh or, occasionally reply something like "Oh! I'm a faerie" (or pixie or dwarf or whatever) letting us know in that case that they are indeed one of our kin. And we accept all otherkind as our kin, although sometimes they are very distant cousins thrice removed.

Traditionally, those who accept the idea of Faerie or Elfland, or Elfin, as we sometimes call it, see it as a parallel realm to our own. Fae folk are considered as Fallen Angels by some, too bad for heaven but not quite bad enough for hell (Evans-Wentz, 1966); or as the dead who now exist around us but in a ghost-like form as the ancient Celts saw us (Arlisson, 2005); or as a species on a similar but slightly different evolutionary line of development from humanity who are above the dead in vibrational tone and can only be seen by certain highly evolved psychics (Charters, 2008).

All these views tend toward the idea of Faerie as a connected but parallel world to our own, less material in the way that fire or air is somewhat less material, but very real. However, it might be more apt to see Faerie as a vibration frequency of our world, in the same way that there is Ultra-Violet or Infra-Red light that most of us cannot see without aid of mechanical devices, or like the high pitched sounds that dogs can hear but most humans cannot, or even radio waves that we cannot pick up without the proper receptor (although occasionally a person's dental filling has been known to pick up signals). These things exist, they are all around us, but because they are not within most people's perceptual range they are not seen and therefore generally ignored. Still most people will acknowledge the idea that Ultra-Violet exists but have yet to yield to the idea of Faerie as a dimensional reality, or the notion that there are beings who exist and function in these usually unseen or unheard realms. On the other hand, shamans and other magic workers through the ages have used various techniques to enter, see, and explore these realms and use them to affect changes in their life and the world around them (Harner, 1982).

At the same time, there are individuals who trace their ancestry through the Celts and other cultures and believe they are the genetic descendants of the ethnic folk who were once known to thems'elves and others as Elves or Faerie folk in one form or another (Gardner, 2003; de Vere, N. 2004). You can find both of these themes in Tolkien's *Lord of the Rings* trilogy. On the one hand the elves leave Middle Earth to another but, in a sense, connected realm. On the other, some elves stay behind because of the love of humanity and clearly contribute genetic material to the human race. We will explore both of these themes, elves as otherworldly creatures and elves as manifesting as a race connected to but different than man, in this book. We accept both these ideas, that there are elves who live in dimensions that are more subtle but still related to our own and that there are elves manifesting among humanity. However, we also go a bit further and propose that is not necessarily or always a matter a genetics, but of choice and spirit.

In the first case, we posit the idea that our Unconscious, which contains everything we've experienced, encountered and know but have forgotten, is also our link to all that we do not know, have not experienced or encountered directly. We are linked, vibrationally, to the all of life and our Unconscious is the radio that can receive the vibrations that wash over us. The difficulty with the unconscious is that it is just that, unconscious, and thus for the most part inaccessible to us. However, it is not totally so for we know that we can remember things we have forgotten and we can learn about things through our imaginal abilities and intuition that we do not directly know, which is the basis of such things as Remote Viewing.

In the other case, we will explore the significance of our mythic or fantasy life to our *real* life and like Jung, posit the idea that the merging of these two elements in a positive way increases our health and psychic wellbeing. This is, in part, what he meant by his term Individuation. One of the means to connecting to the unconscious and the manifestation of the mythic is our imaginal facility, one of the traditional shamanic tools for exploration of the nether, otherworlds or shamanic realms (Harner, 1982).

This thesis then was an exploration of the unconscious elements of Zardoa's psyché utilizing the personal myth as a container, setting and agreed upon symbolic language for communicating between the conscious and unconscious. This thesis had the dual purpose of examining the personal myth as a reflection upon the workings of the psyché, while simultaneously studying its affectivity as a process of Depth or Jungian Inquiry. However, when we relate Faery to the Unconscious, we do not mean to indicate that it exists exclusively as an aspect of the Unconscious, or that the Unconscious is the only means of relating to it. Again, using our analogy of a radio, radio waves do not exist exclusively within the radio; rather the radio is the means of picking up those waves.

Another, perhaps more accurate analogy might be to compare our Unconscious to a library. Our personal library (unconscious) has thousand of books stored within it that we can access by looking them up (if we can in fact find them, which as most of us know is sometimes a bit difficult). Our personal library contains all the information that exists in our unconscious and conscious minds. But, there are also other libraries to which we can connect and from which we can borrow books we don't have in our library. We might, as many esotericists have through time, call this the Akashic library or

Akashic Record (Gray, 1992) that stores the imprint of all that has happened throughout the Universe through time, which can be compared to Jung's idea of the Collective Unconscious. Our ability to access that information, just as our ability to access our Unconscious, depends a great deal upon our development as soulful spirits. This is reflected by various exoteric and esoteric organizations in their grades or degrees. In government, one has various levels of information access, secret, top secret, etc. In the Masons, there are three primary degrees of initiation (and 30 other degrees) that open one to increasing levels of availability to the secrets of that organization. Crowley's orders of the S. S., R. C., and G. D. each offer increasing availability to magical and esoteric knowledge and experience (Crowley, 1976).

These however are merely indications of what should be reality. The truth is there are only two things that limit our access to information and knowledge of the Universe. The first is our real ability to obtain that information via our psyché, our genuine level of adeptship; and the other is our own inclinations as spirits. Just as we filter information coming in to our awareness by our interests, so do we limit/filter our exploration of the Universe according to our interests and predilections.

In pursuing this topic, Zardoa used a qualitative research model based upon Depth Inquiry process techniques. (Depth Inquiry means research that specifically includes the subconscious or unconscious as aspects of the inquiry or subject thereof.) These included Active Imagination, Dream Work, and what we call the Living Dream in which everyday reality was examined as though it was a dream. All these techniques however, were used and focused within the guiding lens of the Personal Myth. That is to say the Personal Myth as a reflection of the unconscious' view of itself was treated with respect and assumed to be, from Shamanic point of view, not mere fantasy, but a truth of its own inner world. This truth, which is the personal myth, was

19

then given life by living it, which is to say, by enacting the personal myth in everyday life.

Since Zardoa's personal myth is centered around the mythology of his Celtic and pre-Celtic/Elven ancestors who believed in a world and people called Faerie or Elfin, the tools of the Tarot, I Ching and other divinatory processes were utilized, and, within the personal myth, accepted as being valid communications with the Otherworld. The Celts and pre-Celtic Pict-Sidhe folk did not have the Tarot or I Ching, of course, but they surely had other means of divination of which these are somewhat modern equivalents. By this we don't mean that they were created in the modern era; the Tarot is, at least, eight centuries old and the I Ching dates back at least four thousand years, but they are still in use and popular in current times. He did not, for instance, wish to cut up an animal and observe how its intestines poured out as some ancient cultures did as a means to foresee the future. We are civilized elves, after all.

The use of these tools involved the suspension of doubt and the acceptance of the idea that the psyché, and the mythic aspect of the individual, while tending to speak symbolically, are real communications from the unconscious of the individual and that the Tarot and other divinatory tools represent, again via symbolic communication, real messages from the unknown/unconscious, the great Universe and in this case from Faerie.

The Otherworld or Faerie is thus seen as being accessible through the unconscious, or really, the unity of the unconscious and the conscious mind. Therefore Faerie, like Zardoa's personal myth, was accepted as being a place or state with its own reality and treated with due respect. We could say that for the sake of this work Faerie was equivalent to Jung's theory of the unconscious, however, it should be noted that the unconscious has access to all things in the Universe, which is vaster and contains more than Faerie, and that Faerie exists in the conscious as well as the unconscious aspects of the

Universe. However, as we pointed out earlier, we are filtering our communications with the Universe, borrowing those books so to speak from the Akashic Library that pertain to Elves, Fae and Faerie.

Zardoa's exploration into the unconscious was opened ended. He communicated with the unconscious using the personal myth and the other tools mentioned above and awaited an answer. Each step in the process was dependent upon the response from the unconscious, and the interpretations of the oracles that were used to reflect it, as to where to go and what to do next. Each step seemed to draw him deeper into the unconscious and it became clear to him that this, indeed, was the very thing the unconscious/Faerie itself wanted, more communication and greater integration with the conscious aspects of the psyché, as well as a place to express itself fully in the conscious world. The tools chosen were particularly suited to this endeavor since oracles, by their very nature, provide seemingly random replies to our questions without the sort of bias, for instance, that one would expect if one sought advice from one's friends or family. One gives them meaning, or finds meaning in them, through what Jung called synchronicity or meaningful coincidence (Jung, 1960a). As a side note, we should point out the Jung hims'elf wrote the forward for the Wilhelm/Baynes translation of the *I Ching*.

Curiously, although the processes of Active Imagination and Dream Work demand a great deal of effort and concentration, at least until you master the techniques, Zardoa found, overall, that his interaction with the unconscious, using the personal myth, was incredibly invigorating. His unconscious responded eagerly to being taken seriously and treated with respect, and its overall message to him indicated a desire on its part for more interaction and integration with the conscious realm of being. Finally, he came to feel that the personal myth as a process of communicating with the unconscious and a method for integrating the psyché, demonstrated, at the very least, that it deserves further and deeper consideration and study.

Some people say that the elves are wise,
but the elves merely claim
to be lovers of truth,
beauty and all that is
wondrous and magical in the world.

CHAPTER 1:

MY MYTHIC ELVEN LIFE

"WHAT DO SO MANY OF US WISH TO BRING BACK TO CIVILIZED AWARENESS IN A MORE POTENT, ALIVE WAY? MYSTERY, INTUITION, RITUAL, RELATIONSHIP, HEALING, EMOTION, SOUL, COMMUNITY, IMAGINATION. IMPORTANT PARTS OF WHO WE ALL ARE. THE STUFF OF MAGIC AND MAGICAL PEOPLE." (WILLIAMSON, 1997, P. 240)

How I Came to this Study

This is a study of my individuation, which is to say the process of becoming a whole person whose unconscious and conscious elements are integrated as well as becoming a unique individual, through the development of my personal myth and the use of that myth as a tool of exploration into the domain of the unconscious. We should note that Jung believed such development to be particularly individual in nature and thus did not believe in the efficacy of group therapy (which in our experience is often based on what Silver Flame [personal communication] refers to as the "lemon squeeze" process, which is to say everyone in the group gangs up on a particular individual and *calls them on their shit*. This was certainly the case with Fritz Perls' Gestalt Therapy and also what Zardoa experienced in Transactional Analysis groups, including his participation in such a group composed of about 40 inmates when he visited Marion Federal Penitentiary. It was also, in part, how the Sorcery Group, which the core sisterhood of the Elf Queen's Daughters evolved into, functioned, which could at times make them seem somewhat cultist, although this is, as we said, a well established and frequently used group therapy method.).

By Personal Myth, I mean an understanding of the self that incorporates the symbolic, imaginal and fantasy elements of the unconscious and accepts them as real within their own realms of being. It is my belief that the Personal Myth is the unconscious' understanding and view of the individual and of the individual spirit's Cosmic/Mythic aspirations and potentialities. It is, in a sense, the personality of the unconscious and of the individual's spirit.

Before we proceed into a discussion of what personal myth is and what my personal mythology entails, I wish to reveal to you some of the experiences which led me to the Depth Psychology Program and how I came to embrace my myth and live it, rather than to continue to repress or suppress it as I, and most other folks, had been enculturated to do. (I should note that the Living of my Personal Myth began long before the Depth Program but that program gave me tremendous understanding of that process and the psychological factors involved.)

In 1972, I received a Master's degree in Speech Communications from Southern Illinois University. I thought at the time that I was finished with the academic community and would never enter that world again. Instead, I entered the world that is popularly called the occult and have received training in and have studied esoteric teachings from all over the world (I did not, however, as some folks do, go all over the world to study them. That was, alas, beyond my financial wherewithal; however, if Mohamed can't go to the mountain, the mountain it turns out, will come to Mohamed.). In the decade before entering the Depth Program, I made my living as a professional fortune teller, reading tarot cards and palms and astrology charts for the public both for a national psychic phone line for 5 ½ years and at a local flea market every weekend for 15 years, and have in my life done over 75,000 tarot readings. I am making no scientific claims here for the efficacy of fortune telling; however, as I proceed, I will reveal how the use of fortune telling or divination has been an integral part in my personal myth, and thus this thesis.

My wife, Silver Flame, has a Master's Degree in Educational Psychology and is the author, under the name Martha Char Love with her colleague Robert W. Sterling of a book of Somatic and Depth Psychology entitled *What's Behind Your Belly Button?*. In 2001, she saw a flyer about the Depth Psychology Program at Sonoma State University. At the time, we didn't even know what Depth Psychology was. As it turned out it was the study of the unconscious of the individual, following the theories of C. G. Jung, Freud, the Object Relations theorists and others. We attended a meeting about the program during which several current students enthusiastically told us how synchronicities keep occurring in their life due to the program. Synchronicities, which we shall explore in more depth later, are essentially coincidences that strike the individual as meaningful (Karcher, S., 1997). In my mind, as I will explain as we proceed, synchronicities are the same as magical occurrences. They are, in fact, the manifestation of magic both in esoteric understanding and common parlance. While my wife, being a devoted student of psychology, was intrigued by Jung's theories; I, being a student of esoteric philosophies and being what might be called a practicing, although I'd say active or performing or even participating, magician of the occult sort, was very intrigued by the idea that something magical might be happening in relationship to the program.

At the same time, I am also a scientist, of a sort, or scientifically minded, and my entry into the world of magic and esoteric teachings has always been moderated by my training as a scientist with a liberal dose of skepticism. Even as a child I was a tad skeptical of superstitious beliefs. When my mother told me, at about age three or four, that we shouldn't open an

25

umbrella in the house because it would create a leak in the roof, even at that tender age, supposedly prior to the age of reasoning, I found that statement extremely suspect.

Therefore, although the students' claims of synchronicity caught my attention, I did not necessarily believe that their reports of their experiences were necessarily accurate or unbiased. They could easily have been of the nature of wishful thinking or self-fulfilling prophecy. (At the same time we might note that self-fulfilling prophecy is one of the goals of magic, certainly Elven Magic, see our book *the Elven Way*.) However, an event occurred which convinced me that there was indeed some validity to their claims, and on the basis of that event, I consented to enter the Depth Program with Silver Flame.

The event that happened was as follows. Facilitating the Depth meeting was the director of the program, Dr. Laurel McCabe. We had never met her before in our lives and did not expect to see her again any time soon. However, the very next evening we had been slated to read fortunes and sell used costume clothing at a dance festival taking place at the local community center. As we set up our booth, the dancers began arriving, and among them was Dr. McCabe who had been studying African dance. The moment I saw her enter the door, I knew that I was being directed by Spirit or, if you will, the Divine or Magic, to enter the Depth Program. This was also a perfect example of a synchronicity, a coincidence that took on personal meaning for me, that is, which I took to be a sign from the spiritual forces that help guide my life.

Early Understanding

I was very young when I first began to sense that I was different from most people. From as early as I can remember I loved girls and began a relationship with my first girlfriend when I was two to three years old. (You may find that hard to believe but it is true.) However, this was not what led me to understand that I was different, for I assumed, at that time, that every boy loved girls as much as I did. However, what distinguished me from most boys at my age was my gentle nature and my lack of interest in sports. This lack of interest was reinforced by my experiences. (Certainly, some elves and fae like sports. There is surely nothing wrong in our minds with doing so. In fact the tales of faery folk playing Hurley in Ireland are quite traditional ((Evans-Wentz, 1966; Green, C. E., Lenihan, E., 2004).). Yet, almost all elfae [elves, fae and otherkin] experience a sense of alienation from the culture and world around them in their early lives.)

When I was about five years old, the local boys encouraged me to go with them up to the neighborhood Catholic school (that I would in a couple of years be attending) and try out for the baseball team. I had no interest in baseball, but I loved playing with the other kids. Although my mother looked at me quizzically when I told her I was going, for she already knew I didn't really care about sports, she made no comment other than to ask me if I was sure I wanted to go. My mother understood me better than I knew mys'elf at that point. When I got there we stood with a group of other boys, waiting to be picked for a team. At the end of the selection, I found myself standing alone. I was never chosen. In fact, the adults in charge of the program never even spoke to me or inquired if I was interested. I watched all the other boys go off together to play and waited for some minutes for someone to speak to me, but no one ever did. Even the boys who had persuaded me to come simply ran off and never said a word to me. This is one of the first signals I received from my peers that I was simply not one of them. It was as though I was an invisible etheric being.

This indication that I was not a sports type was continually reinforced throughout my young life. I was small and slight in build and having no real interest in sports in the first place

27

made no determined effort to acquire the skills that would enable me to participate in sports with any degree of success. I was nearly always the last one chosen for any ad hoc team game and only ever encouraged to play when they didn't have enough players to have a game without me.

One particularly memorable instance of this was when I had graduated from grade school, which for me was a military school (in many ways, rather like Hogwarts), and I returned the following year for the annual graduates versus current student basketball game. Not enough alumni showed up to constitute a team unless I played, and my classmates begged me to participate. So I did, running up and down the court without a clue as to what to do, and the one time I did get the ball, dribbled it off my foot. Fortunately, another of our classmates arrived mid-game and replaced me, but I found the whole experience humiliating and once again swore off the world of sports. The feeling that I was not like the others around me was profoundly reinforced. (The exception to this lack of sports enthusiasm concerned martial arts and so later in life I found mys'elf obtaining brown belts in Karate and Judo. I was never good at either of them, but found them to be both good exercise and interesting.)

You might ask what I was interested in, and the answer to that, which will become increasingly relevant as we proceed, was that I loved to play make believe. I would watch movies or television shows of cowboys or pirates or whatever, and go forth and play that role. I lived in a world of fantasy, and a most wondrous world it was.

Psychotherapist and Jungian analyst D. Stephenson Bond (1993, p. 1) in his book *Living Myth* writes, "A living myth is in many ways a fantasy that has become a way of life. ... the most vital aspect of mythology is not found in the stories of gods and goddesses of long ago, nor in the psychological truths those stories reflect, but rather in the contemporary framework of images and meaning that are found in our own life-styles."

At this point in my life, my myth had not become my life-style; yet, at that very young age, was very close to being so. That is to say, that I was aware that my fantasies were not reality or not of consensual reality, and at that time, while I lived within my imagination a good deal of the time, I made no attempt at that point to integrate my fantasies with that reality, but that would soon come.

However, before we enter my fantasy world and from that my personal myth, let me tell you of other events that increased my sense of alienation not only from other boys, but also from my entire family.

Although I loved girls, and adored my older sister, she, unfortunately, despised me from my birth and according to my mother would pinch me when I was in the crib in fits of sibling jealousy and a terrible feeling, surely, of having been replaced as the cherished center of my father's attention. In later years, it was discovered she had a hormonal imbalance and spent some time in the hospital to correct it, but when I was small, this was unclear to my parents. What was evident, however, was that my sister would fly into rages and beat on me, and she was quickly beginning to outweigh me. When I was in the third grade I was sent away to Linton Hall, a military school run by Benedictine nuns, for the next six years. (I have often compared those nuns to the Bene Gesserit sisterhood of the *Dune* novels, for, like the Bene Gesserit, they also had the power of *the Voice*. When they used a certain tone, we boys knew it was time to straighten up, settle down, and quit pushing at the outer limits.)

At the time, I had no idea why I was being sent away. It was not until much later in my life that my father told me that they had sent me there because they were afraid my sister might kill me. (This theme of a young prince/princess hidden to save hir (his/her) life is often seen in fiction as well as fact and is part of the story of C. S. Lewis' Narnia novel *Prince Caspian* as well as the early life of Jesus.) When I was young and being sent off, he told me simply that it would be good for me. I was also told no toys were allowed at the school (which in actuality turned out not to be true), and I remember thinking that he must be crazy to send me to a place that didn't allow toys. There were about 200+ students in the school each year, and about one nun for every 30 to 40 boys. I think it is fair to say, that for the most part, I was raised by boys. Or as I now tend to see it, raised by pixies.

This situation created an increasing alienation from my family. I spent eight and a half months each year living at military school and only seeing my family from 9 am to 6 P.M. every other Sunday, except those detested Sundays that periodically occurred between January and April when twenty-foot snow drifts and icy Virginia back roads would isolate us from the rest of the world. Six years of family experience and bonding were lost to me. I never felt completely a member of my family ever again, which, on reflection, is probably what saved me from a life of utter dysfunction and enculturated normality and instead helped launch me on the road toward individuation. I could complain about this loss in my life, but I choose instead to incorporate it into my personal myth.

The first summer after I had graduated from military school and was living back home again I nearly had a nervous breakdown. I was in the midst of puberty, and I was unused to the continual pressure of being corrected by my parents about every action or inaction I took. I was soon blinking constantly and clearing my throat to the point that I was afraid I would never be able to stop doing so. Fortunately, this passed, and the feelings of s'elf worth that had developed in my years at military school, as I rose from Private to Captain, and won metals and a trophy, resurfaced within me. This, despite the fact that my father was continually pointing out other boys and forever telling me I should be more like them.

Military school increased my feelings of being different, and it reinforced my sense of alienation from others but it also gave me a sense that my difference, in large part, was due to being special and exceptional as a person. In the next four years, as I lived at home and went to high school I found myself among strangers. Most of the other students had known each other from grade school and were fast friends, having already formed themselves into a variety of cliques. I was continually aware of being a "stranger in a strange land" (Wilhelm, 1967).

I felt alienated from my family. I felt alienated from those around me. As I proceeded through high school, college and graduate school, though I did have friends, I never felt that I could count on anyone. Deep in my heart I've always felt utterly abandoned and alone. This alienation increased as my plans to go on for a Doctorate were squashed by a lack of funds and the dissolution of my first marriage (I had gotten married just prior to entering Graduate School), which affected me deeply.

One afternoon I fell apart emotionally. A young woman had come to visit to get a tarot reading (I have been reading Tarot cards, or in popular parlance fortune telling cards, since my mother bought me my first deck when I was about eight years old). At the time I did the reading for this woman, I didn't actually believe in the tarot, that is to say in their potential accuracy, but I found it interesting, and discovered that I had an aptitude for reading the cards. (In fact, reading fortunes is one of the few areas in my life where I consistently received positive feedback and encouragement.) In the midst of this young woman's visit, my alienation, feelings of abandonment and frustration at my predicament in the world overwhelmed my mind with emotion, and I suddenly stepped out of my trailer and began babbling to the sky. I apologized to the Great Mother for having abandoned her for the world and its semblance of rationality and swore I would never do so again. A few moments later, my acquaintance took me by the hand, guided me back inside to my bed and gave me a much needed, and deeply appreciated and healing, mercy fuck. In fact, at this very moment, dear sister of the stars I continue to send you thanks and blessings.

31

Bond (1993) writes, "...whether or not the eruption of powerful internal experiences turns out to be a breakdown or a breakthrough depends upon the ability of the person to give it form and meaning, upon the ability to mythologize" (pp. 65-66). To my mythic mind, I had been answered by the Goddess. She had heard my call and had sent one of her priestesses to succor me. Hillman (1997) writes, "To what does the soul turn that has no therapists to visit? It takes its trouble to the trees, to the riverbank..." (p. 88). And in my case to the sky.

This was a particularly numinous experience for me. While I did not lose my mind, nor utterly abandon rationality because of this experience, I increasingly embraced my personal myth from that point on. By personal myth I mean my own view of my life as experienced in a subjectively meaningful way, regardless of whether that experience agrees with the common or consensual view of reality. Bond (1993) writes, "Personal myth begins precisely at the moment you say, 'this is vital to me'" (p. x). In a world which had seemed to be incredibly cold and devoid of meaning, I began to find purpose in life and accept experiences that others would think mere fantasy, and these were the seeds of my personal myth as well as my true spiritual life, which eventually would lead me to the Elf Queen's Daughters and the beginning of the acceptance and understanding of my elven, otherworldly nature.

However, before I begin to explore my personal myth and the cultural roots from which it springs, it might be helpful if I define a few terms for you. This is a book examining personal myth from a depth psychology perspective. In order to make my personal myth accessible and understandable, I will from time to time also present the myth from the inside, that is to say from the logic and perspective of that inner world. In doing so I will use different terms according to the perspective from which I am speaking. I will use the vocabulary of Depth Psychology when viewing the Depth aspects of the myth, and I will use the vocabulary of my own myth when speaking from its point of view. In many cases, these terms, while on the

32

surface seeming different because they are the terminologies of two different worldviews, will be used interchangeably. The following list will elaborate these terms.

Definition of Terms

For the sake of this book, the following words should be considered as essentially synonymous. By the word Numinous, which C. G. Jung used to describe something profoundly meaningful or of tremendous spiritual importance for the individual, (Jung, 1983) I will mean essentially the same thing as when I use the term Enchantment. However in using the term Enchantment I will mean not only experiencing the numinous but also acting to promote or create that experience, thus making enchantment an act of magic. In the first instance, one is experiencing enchantment as when one says, for instance, I'm enchanted to meet you or I find this evening very enchanting; and in the other one is creating enchantment; one is the enchanter.

Jung, the psychotherapist who was the primary theorist of Depth Psychology, (1983) tells us, "A great many ritualistic performances are carried out for the sole purpose of producing at will the effect of the numinosum by means of certain devices of a magical nature..." (p. 239). Thus, in using the word Enchantment we do mean that very act of will/magic that strives to produce the numinous. Therefore every attempt an individual makes to contact the spiritual realms of life or make a more meaningful life for themselves or others is defined, in this study, as an act of enchantment or elven magic.

Jung used the word Unconscious to describe a realm of psychological being. The unconscious designates all the parts of our psyché of which we have no conscious awareness (Jung, 1959). It contains all the elements of our being we have

33

repressed or suppressed or have forgotten, which reside in the personal unconscious. It also contains the instinctual drives and archetypal forms of behavior that have been inherited via the collective unconscious. I may use the words Faerie, Elfin, Elfland, Elphame, and the Shamanic Otherworld, while speaking of my personal myth but I will, in part, mean the same thing as Jung does by the Unconscious. Jung (1956) noted a danger of becoming utterly overwhelmed by the contents of the unconscious, which would lead potentially to a psychotic break with consensual reality. Thus entry into the unconscious is to be done with proper guidance, limits and caution. We will see that the same is true of Faerie.

Thus, Tolkien in his scholarly essay *On Fairy-Stories* called Faerie "a perilous land", and states that "in it are pitfalls for the unwary and dungeons for the overbold" (1977, p. 11). Both the unconscious and Faerie are conceived of as mysterious realms that can be potentially dangerous if not approached with the proper caution and the correct attitude. Note that this is the very danger that is cautioned against when one uses psychoactive drugs and the guidelines of having a proper *set* (mindset or attitude) and *setting* (environmental atmosphere and companions) are essential to their use (Leary, T., 1995). Because of this similarity, I am for the sake of this study using these terms synonymously. Thus if I say I am entering Elfin or Faerie, I am at the same time saying I am entering into communication with the unconscious realms of my psyché.

Jung (1959) used the word Self to refer to the complete psyché of the individual combining both the conscious and unconscious aspects of their being. The Self is conceived of as being the totality of the individual's psyché in contrast to the ego, which forms a part of the Self as the individual's conscious awareness. Larsen (1996) tells us that the "... self is to be entered as the fairy realm of myth and folklore..." (p. 105). The word elf will be used here in its highest sense as a more evolved form of humanity, which is to say a humanity that is composed of integrated individuals. I will in many cases substitute the

34

word s'elf as a reminder that these words are being used interchangeably.

The Transcendental Function (Jung, 1971) will be considered the same as the word magic. The transcendental function is the merging of the opposite poles of a person's being, which is to say the conscious and unconscious elements of the psyché, bringing about a more integrated individual. However, magic will also bear with it the idea of conscious individuation or the effort to individuate. In terms of this study, magic will be defined, in part, as any effort of an individual to become whole and to truly know whom they are, to become a whole individual, to know, express and live as their true s'elf.

It should also be noted that while the Numinous and the Transcendental Function are seen as different in Jungian terms, the terms Magic and Enchantment are linked in that both these terms indicate an effort or action whose goal is to integrate the psyché of the individual. This also is an indication that from the point of view of my personal myth, the Transcendental Function most often occurs in a moment of Numinous realization.

From here we will proceed to the psychological literature that will illuminate the current views on the evolution, meaning and value of the personal myth.

"The elves say the tree of life is a forest."
—*ancient elven knowledge*

Elves nearly always recognize other fae
when we encounter them.
But normal folk merely see us as something strange
that they only wish to see
from the corners of their eyes.

CHAPTER 2:

REVIEW OF THE LITERATURE

> *"PAINT ME THY LANDSCAPES, O FAERIE: UNROLL THY*
> *CANVAS FOR EVER. HERE IS A WORLD TO THE EYE:*
> *BUT WE EAT FRUIT OF TRANSFORMATION, AND LO*
> *THERE IS ANOTHER WORLD — ALL OF THY MAKING."*
> *(WAITE, 1974, P. 165)*

The Failure of Cultural Myth

Myth is of little significance to me when considered as a mere fable, but becomes vital when it is activated within my own life. This fact becomes even more relevant when I am not merely experiencing the myths that I have inherited but am actively participating in their ongoing creation, which is to say living my personal myth.

Many scholars (Feinstein, Granger, Krippner, 1988) feel that the cultural myths of the past have lost their power in society and thus have lost their ability to help individuals through life crises (see the Appendix for our ideas concerning a new emerging mythos). They suggest that individuals increasingly fill this vacuum as they create their own personal reality. I find mys'elf in the unique position of having a cultural myth that has not faded but which has been long considered merely a fairy tale or a fantasy connected to a culture that most people think never actually existed. The fact that these tales sprang from stories about real ethnic groups that truly believed in them and other groups that were their inspiration has been lost to the awareness of most individuals in modern society.

Faery Tale

My personal myth is in the form of a literal faery tale, which I am, in part, creating as I go along. Here I'm using Faery Tale in the sense that Tolkien (1977a) does, which is to say a story involving elves or faeries or the magic of the Realm of Faerie. He makes this clarification to distinguish it from folk tales which are commonly called faery tales by Jung's protégé Von Franz (1977) and others but which do not involve Elfin or Faery/Fairy/Faerie magic. Faery tales share with myth the secondary meaning of something that is fictitious. However, they are to be distinguished from myth in two primary ways.

First, not all myths involve the magic of Faerie, and second, myths specifically involve the primordial or archetypal characters that inform the life of a culture or individual (Soukhanov, 1984). For my personal myth thus to be more than just a faery tale it must in someway involve archetypes that have a universal or cultural relevance. My myth then must have meaning and application not only for my life, but for others' lives as well. This is, in fact, the case, because the living of my myth serves as an example for others to live theirs (Hillman, 1997). While my life is a living Faerie Tale, it is one that is mythic in its manifestation. Thus, one does not have to be or think thems'elves an elf or faerie to live their personal myth or find these techniques useful. In fact, it is only by living one's own personal myth, whatever that might be for the individual, that one will find the numinous power and meaning that integration of the personal myth entails. Part of the difficulty of living in the modern world is that one often feels compelled to live a life or myth that is not of one's own choosing and the result of this is a draining of one's psychic energy rather than an empowerment of one's life and spirit.

Personal Myth

Feinstein and Krippner (1997) view the personal myth as "a constellation of beliefs, feelings, images and rules -- operating largely outside of conscious awareness -- that interprets sensations, constructs new explanations, and directs behavior" (p. 5). They assert that by becoming aware of the unconscious myths that direct our lives, such as an Oedipal myth, we can transform them to create more effective and successful means of interacting with our worlds both inner and outer. They assert that personal myths are central to our lives and "tend to be self-fulfilling" (p. 9). And that much of our personal psychological suffering and distress comes from having personal myths that fail to meet our real "needs, potentials and circumstances" (p. 9). In other words, our personal myth exists whether we embrace it or not and influences our lives. However, if we don't develop an awareness of and relationship with our personal myth, and guide it toward positive aspects of being and evolution, we tend to suffer for it.

It is as one transforms the myth into a conscious aspect of one's being that one's myth becomes real, becomes truly lived. By doing so one is enabled "...to seek wisdom from [one's] ... psychological and spiritual depths..." (Feinstein, Krippner, 1997, p. 14) and also "... to receive inspiration from the wisest people and images around [one]..." (p. 14).

Active Imagination, which is a fundamental part of this thesis, is one means of entering one's myth and connecting with inner spiritual resources. Active Imagination is an imaginal process during which one enters into dialogue with one's unconscious (Jung, 1989). And as the myth becomes real, as it begins

39

helping us make sense of the inchoate mass of information and experience that we encounter in daily life, we also begin to recognize, via a sense of the numinous, those wise individuals and images which hold potency for our life (Bond, 1993). I will demonstrate this tendency as I enter the active imaginal part of this book, where I interact with my personal myth.

D. Stephenson Bond (1993) in *Living Myth* tells us, "All too often myth is thought of as the curious stories of curious peoples long gone or far away. Myth is usually someone's else's myth." (p. 1). Thus we have the work of Joseph Campbell (1949) speaking of the myths of various cultures around the world and the work of Jane Shinola Bolen (1984) describing how the ancient Greek mythological figures can arise within our own psychés. However, Bond (1993) writes, "... the most vital aspect of mythology is not found in the stories of gods and goddesses of long ago, nor in the psychological truths those stories reflect, but rather in the contemporary framework of images and meaning that are found in our own life-styles." (p. 1). It is exactly this point of view that is the theme of this book.

Two Types of Thinking

Jung (1956) distinguishes between two types of thinking which he calls "directed thinking and dreaming or fantasy-thinking" (p. 18). Directed thinking works with our elements of speech whose purpose is communication and entails great effort. Dreaming or fantasy-thinking is achieved without effort, arising spontaneously, and is guided by unconscious motives. The first is adaptive in nature, copying reality and striving to alter it with innovations. The other turns its back on reality to set free the subjective tendencies and has no intention nor purpose as an adaptive function, although there are those who believe it to be compensatory in nature, making up for those things we seem to be missing in the outer world, an attempt to bring our psyché into balance. This is certainly Jung's and other's idea concerning dreams as an aspect of wishful thinking, but as we've indicated wishful thinking is a form of magic. (There has been a research study indicating that dreams are not compensatory (Domino, 1976, pg. 658-662).)

The living myth comes from this second style of thinking, and while it shares with fantasy thinking the propensity to be effortless, it can also be empowering. It is not, however, without its dangers. Jung (1956) warns us, "This latter form [dreaming or fantasy thinking], if not constantly corrected by adapted thinking, is bound to produce an overwhelmingly subjective and distorted picture of the world." (p. 28). This is the case in schizophrenia when the contents of the unconscious have overwhelmed the reality oriented directed thinking of the conscious mind. Bond (1993) writes, "In fact, I can get 'lost' in fantasy, 'drown' in fantasy, become overwhelmed by fantasy" (p. 23). When the fantasy becomes too far removed from consensual reality, it becomes dysfunctional. This is why, as I proceed, I will make a case for the importance of the living myth arising out of real experience. That is to say, having the personal myth's contents, for the most part, based upon real experiences.

The Third Alternative

However, we are offered a "third alternative" to getting lost in the imaginal/fantasy realms or living exclusively in the world of the directed or directing mind (Bond, 1993, p. 17), what in the terminology of some magical traditions is called *standing between the worlds* (Matthews, 1996). Bond (1993) calls this third alternative symbolic consciousness. It participates in the inner fantasy realm without losing touch and awareness of the directed thinking of consensual reality. Standing between the worlds does not refer to a place that is in neither this world nor that, but rather a way in which we stand having a foot in each world. In this way, one is able to live within the myth and yet know it to be a myth, which is to say know how it diverges from consensual views of reality. The fantasy is seen neither as reality nor is it seen as illusion but rather Bond (1993) tells us, it is seen as meaning. In this way, one does not lose touch with consensual reality and potentially slip into schizophrenia or schizotypal/delusional thinking, even if one doesn't agree with the view of the world as shared by the majority of individuals; or as they are known to themselves and to elves, as normals; to witches/wicca, mundanes; and in the Harry Potter world, muggles.

By *standing between the worlds*, I am aware of the consensual reality directed thinking and the private and subjective reality of fantasy thinking. I call it a subjective reality because, while others are not always aware of my inner world, it is real for me. This acceptance of the fantasy world as a real world of its own is a traditional Shamanic point of view (Harner, 1982). This is equivalent to acknowledging that the psyché is also a world of its own, equally valid as the shared world of consensual reality. This way of looking at the world is not a new one, but, in fact, a very ancient one. "Our ancestors lived in a mythological world in which virtually every task, every aspect of life; was regulated by fantasy thinking..." (Bond, 1993, p. 14). It is this way of viewing the world that we will be encountering as I reveal my personal myth.

Making the Myth Real

It is my belief that for the personal myth to be effective, it cannot be mere fantasy, nor stem entirely or even mostly from fantasy. McAdams writes, "We must seek credibility in our life stories. The good, mature, and adaptive personal myth cannot be based on gross distortions. Identity is not a fantasy" (p. 111). That is why, in part, I've entitled this study, *Living the Personal Myth*. For the myth to be viable it must be lived, that is, functional within the world of consensual reality, even if it doesn't entirely agree with the assumptions of that world. My personal myth may hold as true things that are considered fantasy in the normal world, as for instance, my basic animistic belief in the consciousness of all life. That I disagree with the world's assumptions is not important. What is important is that my beliefs are based on real experience and are functional within the world, even if contrary to its currently held assumptions.

However, it is important to note that from a traditional shamanistic standpoint, inner experience is just as real and valid as outer events. Larsen (1996) writes, " As we develop a deeper rapport with our own imagery, it will 'mirror' our concerns at ever - deeper levels..." (p. 53). However, he adds, "The image in the magic mirror, like the ones in fairy tales, gives you a true seeing about yourself, but not necessarily the one you expected or wished to see" (p. 53) (Note that this is the purpose of such oracles as the I Ching that do not necessarily give one the reply one is hoping to receive). The unconscious and the inner realm of myth has its own point of view, which becomes viable, in my opinion, when it is based on actual, rather than entirely fantasized events, in the individual's life.

Let me give you an example. I might fantasize that I am a king. However, that is merely a fantasy and does not have the power that stems from a real event, and thus, as an aspect of my personal myth, it would be impotent. On the other hand, I knew a young man from Thailand, who repeatedly introduced me to his friends as the king. I have no idea what motivated him to do so. However, this act, coming from consensual or lived reality has a great deal more potency to it. It is real, actual and thus more powerful. "Our mythic sensibility may pick up the authentic tidings of inward things, but authenticity can be assured only by checking the facts..." (Hillman, 1997, p. 100).

The truth is my requirement for the elements that compose my personal myth are somewhat more rigorous than that, although I won't go into that now, and I have not, in my own mind, achieved the status of kingship. However, that doesn't alter the fact that there is at least one person (actually there are more, in fact, just yesterday a green haired street pixie referred to Zardoa as the Dragon King, when we passed him by on the sidewalk) who declared me to be a king. This is a fact in the real world, not a product of fantasy.

The Collective Unconscious

The shamanistic view that the inner world of the unconscious and the imaginal are real events is reflected in psychological thinking when Jung (1956, p. 28) asks, "...

whether the mainly unconscious inner motive which guides these fantasy-processes is not in itself an objective fact..." This fact is the "autonomous imagination" (Bond, 1993, p. 23), the fact that our psyché has a life of its own. "In the encounter with the "Not-I," the alien within, the collective unconsciousness becomes not an idea, but a relationship" (Bond, 1993, p. 24). If all of life is alive, as our animistic thinking ancestors believed, than an encounter with the collective unconsciousness is, from their point of view, a relationship with them, the very ancestors from whom we inherited this collective unconscious. They give us a very real knowledge of how to encounter the world.

In this worldview, we need each other, the ancestor and ourselves. They need us to feed their spirits in the Otherworld, the unconscious, and we need their continuing guidance and wisdom (Bond, 1993). It gives continuity to life. "...the need for myth is the need for meaning - meaning as a living relationship. The movement from symbolic consciousness to mythological consciousness comes from the need to live in a context." (Bond, 1993, p. 25). Myth provides meaning for our life, that is to say, it makes our life make sense to us. The personal myth glues together the often seemingly disparate aspects of our lives, into a coherent and purposeful story.

Part of this relationship comes from within us, in the form of a need to relate to our unconscious, but there is also a need to relate to the world about us. Bond (1993) writes, "... myth has to do with the vital necessity of discovering a functional relationship to the environment..." (p. 32). This means living in relationship not only to one's cultural and social milieu but also in relationship to the vital and living earth that supports us, and the trees and other beings that share our world. It is this very idea that is at the heart of aboriginal cultures as well as the evolving literature of Eco-Psychology. (Gomes, Kanner, Roszak, 1995) "Our mythological frame of reference can no longer be the single culture in which we dwell. The scope of our responsibility and our loyalty must move beyond the local social boundary to the planet we inhabit together." (Larsen, 1988, p. 169). McAdams writes that fashioning the personal myth is not an act of delusion but an ongoing process of "psychological and social responsibility" (p. 35). We are not separate elements in a disconnected world but individual aspects of an interconnected whole, whose being exists not simply through space, but through time, connecting us to all who have come before us as well as all with whom we currently share this planetary environment.

Culture is generational and is a relationship of identity passed from those now dead to the currently living. This prompts Hillman (1997) to say that the major task of a "life-sustaining culture, then, is to keep the invisibles attached, the gods smiling and pleased..." (p. 112). He tells us this is not a matter of belief nor of superstition, but a basic understanding that without the spirits we have nothing but human beings to "cover our back[s]" (p. 112). And for someone as alienated from and abandoned by humans as I have been, that just won't do.

45

However, culture and myth are not objects, like a book, passed unchanged from generation to generation. Bond (1993) tells us that a living myth could be considered as a "myth - in - process" (p. 35) that establishes a workable relationship between a culture and its environment. McAdams tells us, "Through our personal myths, we help create the world we live in, at the same time that it is creating us" (1993, p. 37). The purpose of the personal myth therefore is not to separate us from each other, nor lead us away from the realities of the consensual world, but to help us integrate what we feel and experience inwardly with what is demanded of us outwardly. This integration of the inner and outer worlds, the integration of our conscious understanding of reality with our unconscious is exactly Jung's prescription for individuation.

The Theory of the Daimon/Dæmon

One might ask, who is this Self that includes both our conscious and our unconscious aspects, our fantasy as well as directed thinking? And who is this "not I" (Bond, 1993, p. 24) that lives within us? Hillman (1997) tells us, "No person is a genius or can be a genius, because the genius or daimon or angel is an invisible nonhuman escort, not the person with whom the genius lives" (p. 29). He informs us that this daimon has affinities to myth, because it is, itself a mythical being whose thoughts are of a mythic nature. It is an archetypal being who has the job of ensuring one becomes who the individual is truly and uniquely meant to be. As McAdams (1983) confirms, "Each of us creates a personal myth that in all its details is like no other story in the world" (p. 50). It is our personal myth that helps define us, give us meaning, makes our life understandable to ours'elves (see definition of terms), if to no one else.

46

Yet living the personal myth has implications beyond the individual, as Hillman (1997) tells us. Those who are to awaken to the power of their own daimon and myth need "living personifications of fantasy, actual people whose lives seem pulp fiction, whose behaviors, speech, dress carry a whiff of pure fantasy" (p. 169). By living the personal myth, we encourage others to do the same. By becoming individuated, we encourage individuation. Thus living one's personal myth is not merely an act of s'elf fulfillment, but, as Bond (1993) told us, an act of social responsibility. In the realm of myth, we are no longer alone, but connected to all who live, all who have ever lived and all who will come to be. I am no longer alienated but part of the great frasority (my word combining fraternity and sorority) of those striving through the ages for a better life and world for all.

We should note that the daimon of Hillman was called a dæmon by the ancient Greeks; however, because it is pronounced demon, and due to the prejudices of early Christianity, these spirits are often confused with such beings. But the daimon/dæmon's purpose is to guide and inspire, it is one's genius, genii, djinn and only becomes demonic when its guidance and messages are ignored. Then it can, like repressed aspects of the unconscious, surge forth in times when one is drunken or under stress to one's great embarrassment.

Living the Myth

As we live mythologically, we "begin to grasp the transcendent, to see it alive in oneself, in one's life, in one's work, friends and environment" (Wilber, 1981, p. 126). By connecting to our personal mythos and the mythos of our particular culture, the creative becomes awakened in our individual lives. We begin to connect to something that is transcendent, that is beyond the narrow sphere of a particular lifetime. We begin to see our lives in the context of the vast movement of creation. It is exactly this connection to the transcendent, this aliveness of the myth that I mean by living the personal myth.

By living our myth we make it real, we make it manifest, not only for ours'elves but for others as well. Hillman (1997) tells us there are "certain necessary nutrients ... that evoke the early imagination..." (p. 160) and one of these is "... that there be odd fellows and peculiar ladies within the child's perimeter..." (p. 160). Thus one of the necessary ingredients for unleashing the imagination of creative individuals, is having eccentrics or those beings who are in fact living their personal myths as an example of the imaginal world made manifest. It is therefore our duty to live our personal myth, to individuate, to heed our calling (Hillman, 1997) and become who we are truly meant to be. And by doing so, by becoming one of those whom Hillman (1997) calls "... living personifications of fantasy..." (p. 169), we become an example for others struggling to find their own unique s'elves.

However, Larsen (1996) observes whenever we become any of the "... dramatis personae of the mythological world, we are dissolved in the archetype. . ." (p. 3) If you wish to observe individuals dissolving in archetypes observe teenagers slavishly imitating the fashions, behaviors and even exact dialogue of their cultural models that they've encountered primarily through the media and other imitators like themselves. Larsen notes that our individuality perishes as we take on these eternal roles and ". . . yet it is only through entering this paradoxical zone that we truly find our individuality" (p. 3).

What can be the meaning of this? How are we to find our true s'elves, if that very s'elf becomes dissolved by the archetype? I contend it is by way of the personal myth that this is done. By individualizing the myth, that is by living it and making it real within our own lives, we give vitality and meaning to the archetypal forms that are the source of that myth. When the universal mythic forms become personalized in our own being, we become in contact not only with the universal, but become a unique aspect of that universal form. It is the personal myth that both connects us to the vast world in which we truly live, the world of the stars, and also allows us to be our own very special individual who is, hopefully, an individuating form of the universe manifest. However, to do this without remaining in touch with the immediate reality of day to day living can have devastating consequences.

To be out of touch with consensual reality is to court delusion and schizophrenia (Bond, 1993). However, are we not also courting a form of madness if we are not in touch with the mythic and universal themes that relate us to the greater world in which we live? Not only the vast, perhaps endless, world of planets and galaxies, but the equally vast inner world of the unconscious psyché whose language is symbolic (Larsen, 1996) and whose life is mythic (Feinstein, Krippner, 1997)?

To understand the power of the daimon or *Calling* as it manifests in the average individual's life, Hillman (1997) argues we can best come to comprehend it by looking at those exceptional individuals for whom the *calling* manifested most strongly. So too, in trying to understand the power of the personal myth, it might be best to understand how it functions in those individuals who so obviously live in their own worlds and personal myths (James; Weeks,, 1996), the eccentrics.

Eccentrics, of all people in the world, make their personal myth real by living it. Rather than conforming to the current modes, fashions and morés of current society, eccentrics inevitably decide for thems'elves how they shall live and dress and what they shall believe. They are those exceptional beings Hillman (1997) points to as being necessary for those in whom the daimon will be heeded.

Eccentrics

After ten years of research on the subject of eccentrics Dr. David Weeks concluded in the findings to his study that eccentrics have an average higher intelligence than the general population, are happier, healthier and thus typically live longer (James; Weeks, 1996). But most interesting of all, Dr. Weeks was most surprised at, ". . . the results we obtained... showing that serious schizophrenic symptoms were actually less common among eccentrics than the general population." (p. 199). While eccentrics are often viewed as strange and mad or insane, they are in fact, for the most part healthier and saner than the general population (James, Weeks, 1996). By becoming in touch with your true S'elf, that is with the totality of your being by individuating, you become not only healthier psychologically, but also physically.

A denial of one's inner world, a denial of the personal myth, where one lives only in the world of consensual reality, the world of the persona, Jung's (Stein, 1998) term for the social role one adapts in order to gain acceptance in society, does not guarantee one protection from neurosis or psychosis. As James and Weeks (1996) point out to us, "In seventeenth century Salem, Massachusetts, the behavioral norm in one notorious period was mass hysteria; anyone who maintained the barest semblance of moderation and humanity was nonconforming." (p. 41). We could as well mention Nazi Germany, and Europe during the time of the witch-hunts as sharing a similar mass madness in which multitudes participated in a participation mystique, in which their personal myths became wholly absorbed by the current cultural myth, which was neither healthy nor sane.

Thus I propose from the results of my research of the literature a two-fold hypothesis. First, that a personal myth that is in touch with or consciously aware of consensual reality is far healthier for the individual than a myth that is out of touch

50

with consensual reality and would be, therefore, potentially disintegrating for the personality. Second, that having a personal myth is far healthier than a lack of personal myth altogether, in which one is wholly absorbed in the cultural mythology. As Joseph Campbell (1968) tells us "Mythological symbols touch and exhilarate centers of life beyond the reach of vocabularies of reason and coercion" (p. 4). We might say, beyond the world of doubt and uncertainty, beyond alienation and sense of meaninglessness. For myth brings meaning into our lives (Bond, 1993; Larsen, 1996); it gives us certainty and purpose; it connects us to our ancestors (Hillman, 1997) and to our environment (Bond, 1993). Through myth we find our place in the world, a place in which each of us is special and has a unique purpose.

And now, at last, let us enter into the world that is the setting for my personal myth.

When men tell us they kill two birds with one stone, we elves always wonder why are they killing birds?

"When the fae get tortured in life, they can come out
to be pretty odd ducks,
but you just have to love them
and they bloom and brighten."
—Silver Flame of the Silver Elves

The way of the elves is quite simple.
They say be yourself,
do your magic in harmony
with Nature and the Divine
and encourage others to do the same.
And all things shall in time turn out perfectly
and as they were always meant to,
which is to say,
as we've ever desired and wished them to be.

CHAPTER 3:

THE DEVELOPMENT OF

MY PERSONAL MYTH

"ALL EARTHLY MELODY SEEMS REMEMBERED ECHOES OF WHAT HAS BEEN HEARD IN FAERIE."
(WAITE, 1974, P. 164).

Welcome to My World

James Hillman (1997), Jungian analyst and the originator of archetypal psychology, argues that the generally accepted opinion, which holds that the parents, particularly the mother, is the most formative power in a person's life, is inaccurate. He offers instead the idea that there is the archetypal daimon who guides us and drives us toward fulfillment of our true nature and calling. This daimon is in the form of a guiding force or guardian angel who holds the image of what we are meant to be. Of this he writes, "Yet all along a little elf whispers another tale: 'You are different; you're not like anyone in the family; you don't really belong.' There is an unbeliever in the heart. It calls the family a fantasy, a fallacy." I heard that elf. It whispered to me: *You are one of us.*

I am an elf. I realize that must sound strange to some readers, since from the popularly accepted point of view, elves are fictional beings who do not and, being a product of fiction/fantasy/fairy tales/folk lore, cannot exist. However, the intelligent reader, like yourself, will ask, what do you mean by that statement? And my reply is multifold. When I say I am an elf, I mean, in part, that I am a theorist and practitioner of what I call the *Elven Way* (see our book of that title), which is a spiritual practice. Therefore, when I say I am an elf, I'm using it in the same way someone might say, I'm a practitioner of Buddhism, or Hinduism, or Catholicism or Judaism.

However, as you will see, for mys'elf, I also use my identification as an elf in both a genetic sense and a cultural one. Thus I could say to you that I am a descendent of the Scottish, English, Welsh, French and Dutch, but as I trace the ancestry of those peoples further back, I find I am equally entitled to tell you I am a descendent of the Pixies, Elves, Brownies, and Fae or Faery Folk. Just as some modern Italians could say they are descended from the Romans and some might argue before that the Trojans, so I tell you I am descended from the folks who were once known as the Elves, Pixies. Brownies and Fae. And just as the stories of Troy where once thought to be purely fictional or mythological until the late 1870's, so are the stories of my ancestors currently considered in just this way.

And I also use the term elf culturally. So when I say I am an elf, I also mean that I carry on many of the traditions and fashions that have been passed on through the ages by my people. However, I don't ask you to believe I am an elf. I simply ask to you to understand and accept that this is the culture, people and tradition, with whom I identify. And it is this culture that is at the heart of my personal myth.

Religion or Culture?

If you tell someone that you are a Buddhist, a Catholic, a Jew or even an agnostic or atheist, while they might not agree with your choice, they at least, for the most part believe it to be a real one. If you tell someone your ancestors were Italian or Japanese or Cherokee or even some tribe from Africa that they've never heard of, they will accept what you say without question. Try telling someone you're an Elf.

If you tell someone you are descended from elves, they will, A. think you're crazy, or B. think you are pulling their leg, or C. think that you have taken Dungeons and Dragons a mite too seriously which brings us back to A.

If you tell someone you are on the Elven Path rather than claiming any other religious affiliation they will think you are, A. crazy, B. pulling their leg, or C. part of a weird cult, which brings us back to A.

Because, in the minds of most people, elves do not and have never existed except in Faery Tales. The very words Fairy Tale is defined by the dictionary (Soukhanov, 1984) as a story that is fanciful or fictitious.

So are we, as elves, a religion and thus some form of new age cult, or are we a culture descended from a people who never existed except in the imagination of fanciful people, and in tales told to children before they are old enough to realize what the world is really like?

The answer is neither. The Elven Path is animistic in nature. Nearly all tales about us say that we are the Elder Race (Evans-Wentz, 1966; Tolkien, 1977b), the original people. Our path is aboriginal and thus, as Frazer (1951/1922) points out, shamanistic and pre-religious. Ours is a spiritual path, not a religion. We have no dogma, doctrine nor specific rituals, although every elf is free to follow whatever religion or believe whatever they choose concerning religion, the Universe and the world.

Is it a path we've inherited or is it one we've created? To me that doesn't matter; for all spiritual paths began somewhere, sometime. All things, all religions, all cultures, are created. So for the longest time I would tell people that if there never were a historical people called elves, there are now! Yet, I always felt,

55

deep, deep within, that I was descended from elves. For who else but elves would even wish to claim to be an elf?

My Ancestors

According to my mother I am descended from the Scottish and from French Huguenots who fled to Wales to avoid persecution for their religion and fled to America in the 1600's to avoid prosecution for horse theft. On my father's side, I'm descended from the Scottish, English and a bit from the Dutch. Who were these people before there was anyone who called themselves Scottish or English or French or Dutch? Laurence Gardner gives us the answer.

The Realm of the Ring Lords

According to the cover of his book *Realm of the Ring Lords*, Laurence Gardner is a "sovereign genealogist and historical lecturer" (2003). He tells us:

The most important aspect of the early Grail successions was the conjoining of their various lines of primary descent... the resultant family was the most prestigious in all history to date. They were the Royal Scyths of the Albi-gens — the line which spawned the fairy kings of the Tuadhe d'Anu. In time, their descendants were the High Kings of the Irish, Picts and Scots, with their legendary links to the Merovingian [French] Fisher Kings and the enchanted dynasty of the Elf Kings. (p. 65).

It is from these peoples I claim descent. From the Pict-Sidhe (pixies), the Merovingian Fisher Kings (the fae or faery folk) and the Albi-gens, the Elven Bloodline. So are modern elves

56

obligated to prove they are descended from the Scots, Picts, etc.? The answer is no, at least not from the point of view of these elves.

The Aboriginal World

Belief in the little folk is not derived exclusively from Europe (Evans-Wentz, 1966) but is to be found nearly worldwide. Malidoma Patrice Some speaks of a belief in elves in his African culture (1998), and J. E. Roth (1997) presents us with an encyclopedia of beliefs among aboriginal Americans concerning the little folk. This includes the Hawaiians who believe the Menehunes or little magical folk lived on the islands before they came.

Immortality

Legends of elves commonly say they are immortal or so long lived to be considered so by normal humans (Tolkien, 1977b). On the other hand, Evans-Wentz (1966) presents us with the possibility that the Sidhe, the Faery Folk, the Elves, are always those who have passed on into the spirit world. They are always the culture that came before. We must remember that our ancestors were animists. In their worldview, everything, every tree, bush, and person, living and dead, was alive, each in their own realm of being.

As I've said, I am also an animist. Everything is alive. I believe in reincarnation, and I believe that elves, having the powers that we do, can incarnate within any culture we chose whether European or not. For the Elven culture is not in its essence a culture of materialism but of spirit. What does it matter where

57

our genes came from? For us, genetic ancestry is but of passing interest. It is from whence our spirit/soul has descended that matters to the elves.

Creating Culture

All culture is created. I make this statement boldly because it seems so obvious to me. Every bit of culture is something someone at some time created by accident or by intention, which somehow resonated in the minds and hearts of others. The seven-pointed acute angled Elven Star for instance, sometimes called the Faerie star, that is used by elfae worldwide was first presented as an elven symbol by the Elf Queen's Daughters in the original *Elf Magic Mail* (see our two books that have reproduced the contents of these letters) and is featured on the covers of Lupa's (2007) *A Field Guide to Otherkin* and Emily Carding's (2012) *Fairy Craft*. These resonant activities, events, thoughts and deeds are then carried on to and by those who did not create them but have instead inherited them. Bond tells us, "Myth is by definition an artifact of a culture, a shared social system of meaning, not usually a personal creation" (1993, p. 29). We elves would argue that it is both personal and shared.

This tradition of inheritance has power so long as it still resonates within the hearts and minds of the inheritors. At the point the resonance fades away the power fades as well. "A myth is alive when it shows a way of life, a life-style, a structure of daily living. A myth has become a fossil when it is no longer a way of life that satisfies" (Bond, 1993, p. 28). In other words, when the myth fails to speak to our life as currently lived, when it fails to inspire us, guide us and fill us with a sense that life has purpose and meaning, the myth fades and dies. We are told (Feinstien; Krippner; Mortifee, 1998), "The old myths that once united us are fading, leaving societies fragmented and

58

disoriented. Can we create a new unifying mythic vision for the future?" (p.5) (For an answer to this question see the Appendix).

Alas, those who have learned and been taught to inherit do not always, perhaps seldom, know how to create. They await a new creator; they await the new creation; they await the new myth. Bond (1993) asks, "How is a culture to renew itself except through individuals who restore the cultural imagination? That is, where do the sustaining myths of culture come but from what were once personal myths in individual lives?" (p. 29).

Perhaps this myth will come by intention, perhaps it will come by accident, but if a culture, and thus a people, is to live, that is to be filled with life energy, power and meaning, the sustaining myth must come. When the myth I had inherited began to fade and die, I reached back, back into the past, back into the collective unconscious, back to the beginning.

In the Beginning Was Santa Claus

The very first mythological figures I encountered in my life were Santa Claus and his elves. Although my parents were Catholic and I was told that Christmas was Jesus's birthday, it was Santa and his elves who brought me presents and were to me, very real. Jesus was merely an ephemeral figure that had no real presence (presents) or meaning in my life. In fact, dear Jesus was the cause of such boring and life draining events such as mass for an hour every Sunday.

I remember at one Christmas my sister, who was a year older than I, revealed that there wasn't really a Santa Claus, doing this not to be cruel, I think, but to demonstrate her superior knowledge; and I must admit that I was shocked to hear this. I was shocked because I couldn't understand why my mother, who told me never to lie, had lied to me. But most of all, I was

59

shocked that someone whom I loved so much was suddenly made to not exist. I wanted Santa to be real, and that desire remained within me.

Of course, the presents kept coming, and every year images of Santa and his elves would adorn the Yuletide world. And so, in a sense, Santa never left me, and I came in time to understand that Santa Claus, while not a physical being was, like Jesus, based upon someone who had once lived and whose spirit went into the world and still holds power there. The difference, however, was that for me Santa resonated deeply within, which is something the figure of Jesus never did.

I came to realize that every one who gave presents in Santa's name (which my parents did every year even after he had been revealed as a mythological figure), were acting as agents for the Spirit of Santa Claus. They were, in fact, his elves creating a world of joy and beneficence for every girl and boy. If I give a gift in Santa's name, am I not, in fact, acting as Santa would act? Have I not become, at least for that moment, the living embodiment of his spirit? Has he not become alive through me, not merely as a myth but as a living myth whose power still holds sway in the world with those who believe most purely, truly and innocently? It is sometimes said that gods die when they are no longer believed in, however, Santa still lives as powerfully and as strongly as he ever did and, as long as I live, he will continue to do so.

There is a powerful aspect of transformation that lives in the unconscious elements of the Santa myth, for it is the myth of giving more than receiving. I know that I began my life as a receiver, expectantly awaiting Santa's coming. I still do, in fact. However, in becoming Santa Claus, in giving for giving's sake, without looking for a reward or a gift in return, I have learned the tremendous joy that comes from seeing happy, excited children. My soul, which hungered so deeply, has been satisfied, time and again, by gales of laughter and squeals of glee. But one seldom learns the joys of giving without having first received, so let me tell you of some of those who first gave to me.

The Forest Perilous

I was standing on the outside of the fence, on the edge of the forest, staring into the backyard of the neighbor who lived immediately across the court from my family. I was only about two years old at the time, and my hero was Hopalong Cassidy. And there, in my neighbor's backyard was a play fort made of logs that resembled the forts in cowboy and cavalry movies. I stared in fascination, longing and hoping to be able to go within it.

On that day there were three little girls (or were they faeries? Reflecting back, I'm not sure.) inside the fort having a make believe tea party. They were each a year or two older than I. Fortunately, my sister, who hated me passionately wasn't among them, for if she had been I'd never have been permitted within. One of the girls spoke to me and invited me in, but I was far too shy to either answer or make a move. Finally, she came out of the yard, took me by the hand and led me back to what was, for me, a dream come true. I was in paradise, in a cowboy fort, surrounded by beautiful girls.

It was not long before the youngest of the three, who was still a year older than I, became my girlfriend. We were constant companions and her sister, who was a year older yet, always made me feel safe and protected when we would encounter other, rougher boys.

There was a forest behind our house and my mother had said, "Promise never to go in there," for unspecified dangers lurked within, dangers whose exact nature I did not know except as concern, whispered and mumbled, just beyond my hearing. She also made me promise "never to lie". However, one day the two sisters invited me to go into the woods with them and assured me it would be all right. So I let them take me by the hand, and we entered the world of wonder that is a forest, a realm that belonged almost exclusively to children, in which few adults ever tread.

Down a dirt path we went, surrounded by trees and leaves and the distant sound of children laughing, until finally the path widened out on the upper bank of a creek bed. The creek seemed to have enormous banks the size of small mountains. Over the creek and hanging from a tree branch a rope with knots in it had been suspended. There the children (or were they pixies?) were wildly assembled, swinging, laughing, shouting and having a wondrous time. I was utterly amazed.

It was rather overwhelming for me. I was but a wee, small and extremely shy child, and they were to my eyes an unruly band of unsupervised wildness. I stared wide-eyed and amazed. Was this what my mother had been so afraid of? Did she even know this world existed? I doubted it, for I had never seen either of my parents enter the forest and presumed they had never done so. This was another world entirely. A world without adults where children ruled, and play was the most important thing in the world. How daring they seemed to me. They flew across the creek holding onto a rope. Where had they come from? I'd never seen any of these kids before. They had come from another realm.

When I returned home I found my mother awaiting me. She asked me where I had been, for she had been calling for me. I neither wished to tell her the truth nor lie to her, so I stood there in utter silence and just stared at her with wide-eyed innocence. Finally, she asked, "Were you hiding behind the couch?" and I nodded that I had been.

For me that day will always stand out in my memory. It was the day that the faery girls led me into the forbidden and perilous forest where the fey folk dwell. It was also the day I learned that deception was far superior to lying. You never had to

62

compromise the truth, you just needed to allow people to believe what they chose to believe.

Why did I go into the forest perilous? It wasn't because I was brave or courageous or heroic. I wasn't on a quest, I wasn't even curious. I was both shy and timid. So why did I go? I went because the faery girls told me it would be okay. In a world in which my sister, for no reason I could understand or perceive, was often hostile and cruel to me, two gentle elf sisters had taken my hand and treated me with kindness. They had taken a lonely boy staring at the rath (elf fort) and embraced him as one of their own. Of course, I went with them. They were magic. The world had come alive for me when I found them, and though I loved my mother and trusted her and always tried to be "the good boy" that she wanted me to be, I trusted the magic more. (For many more stories about our personal myth and the magic of our lives see our book *Eldafaryn: True Tales of Magic from the Lives of the Silver Elves* (2011).)

Changelings

One of the great benefits for me of the personal myth is that it makes my life understandable. Seen as isolated incidents and experiences much of my life has been incomprehensible. However, when I reflect upon my life from the point of view of my personal myth, it all begins to make sense. The personal myth gives a cohesive meaning to my life, and it is in just this way that my myth becomes numinous.

There is a legend about the elves that we would exchange our babies for human babies, raising the human ones among us and leaving ours to be raised by them. Legend has it that the normal folk when they discovered this exchange were advised to cast the Elfin baby into the fire (Evans-Wertz, 1966). Can you imagine what desperation would lead a people to exchange their own babies for another people's, considering that they might be thrown into a fire if discovered? What, but a incredible need to preserve one's people from extinction, could possibly lead a mother to so exchange her child for another's?

When I was about three or four years old, my sister told me that I wasn't my mother's child, but had been found in a pigpen. My mother, I think a bit reluctantly, went along with this teasing for a little while agreeing that I was indeed a child found abandoned in a pigpen.

From a modern point of view we might say that it is not unheard of for older siblings to tease younger ones. And we might speculate that her teasing had been learned from being teased herself. However, when viewed from the perspective of my personal myth, this tale takes on an entirely new dimension. Evans-Wentz (1966) demonstrated in his research a very probable connection between the word pixie and the word Picty. The ancient Picts or Pict-Sidhe (pronounced pict- she) were the faery folk of ancient Alba (Scotland) (Gardner, 2003). In being translated from one dialect to another in the British Isles, Picty becomes not only pixie, but also piskie (a Cornish elf) and pig-sy (Evans-Wentz, 1966).

Am I descended from a changeling, or as we elfin say an ex-changeling? A baby who fell among those too kind to cast it in the fire? Indeed, I am. For in accepting that idea, I come to understand that my sister wasn't being cruel, she was merely speaking a truth she herself did not entirely understand. I am mythically, at the very least, one of the pig-sy, piskie, pixie folk.

The name Alba, the name of ancient Scotland, by the way, is related to the word Albion the ancient name for Britain which means the land of the White Goddess (Graves, 1966/1948). The word Alb has been demonstrated by both Graves (1966/1948) and Gardner (2003) to be connected to the word white, but also in ancient Germanic alb means elf. Thus we might consider that Alba and Albion could be translated equally as the land of the white goddess or the land of the elf goddess, the land of my ancestors.

Losing my Religion

Jung (1989) wrote:

I had explained the myths of peoples of the past; I had written a book about the hero, the myth in which man has always lived. But in what myth does man live nowadays? In the Christian myth, the answer might be, "Do you live in it?" I asked myself. To be honest, the answer was no. For me, it is not what I live by. (p. 171)

After four years at home following military school, during which I attended high school, I went away to college, and except for vacations during this period, never lived at home again. It was during my college period that I became alienated from the Catholic church. I had a friend with whom I would go to mass each Sunday, and often we would walk though a park on the way there. I keep wondering why we didn't hold mass in the park under the trees. It just seemed the right thing to do. Sitting in a church felt unnatural to me somehow. Besides I just didn't believe in the church's teachings anymore. In fact, even as a small boy I had never entirely done so. They preached that thinking about sex (which in my young mind meant kissing girls) was sinful and I just didn't believe this was so.

One Sunday after mass, when I expressed my dissatisfaction with the church and its doctrines, my friend turned to me and said, "Then why do you go?" This struck me like a bolt of lightening, and I wondered to myself, why indeed did I go for I did not really believe, and I never went again, except as a family event when visiting my parents. From that moment on, I spent my Sundays worshiping at the church we fallen Catholics call, St. Mary's of the Mattress.

Curiously, it was just at this point that I added Philosophy and Religion as a major so I eventually graduated with a double major in Speech/Theatre and Philosophy/Religion. So while I had abandoned my religion I had not in the least given up my interests and aspirations in spiritual development. In fact, quite often on weekend nights I would go with several friends to a house in a nearby town, where young members of the Bahai faith would regularly meet. While most of my contemporaries were spending Friday night getting drunk, I was listening to spiritual discourse.

This is not to say that I was eager to join the Bahais. In fact, I was extremely skeptical and argumentative. However, I couldn't help but be intrigued by them and was deeply impressed by their kindness and simple goodness. Even when I graduated and went into a master's program in another state, I found Bahais there and would love to hang out with them. They were good folk.

The EQD

In 1975 I first encountered the Elf Queen's Daughters. The Elf Queen's Daughters (EQD) were practitioners of Wicca or Witchcraft. They identified thems'elves as elves and had centers or vortexes, as they called them in Ohio, Illinois, Oregon, California and a number of other states. I had been working in a vegetarian restaurant that was open only for lunch each day and was sponsored by, and established in the building that housed the Hillel Foundation in Carbondale, IL. On the same floor but around the corner from the restaurant and the rabbi's office was an occult bookstore. Outside the bookstore was a bulletin board, and on it I found two printed letters/flyers from the EQD, giving their address in Aurora, Illinois.

I found the letters intriguing. However, I also sensed that they might be a bit feminist and that if I wrote to them I might not receive as welcome a response as I would if I were female. To test this hypothesis, I asked a girl with whom I worked, who had also seen the letters and found them interesting but was less intrigued than I, to write to the elves at the same time I did, so we could compare the results. The result, as it turned out, was rather surprising, for I received a very enthusiastic reply whereas hers was polite but ho hum. (Later, on a visit to the Aurora vortex, or to the Fox River Elves, as I called them, since they lived on the bank of the Fox River, I asked Melryn, one of the sisters there, why I had received such an enthusiastic letter when my acquaintance had received a somewhat lukewarm response and, in fact, had never written again. Melryn told me, "You letter was filled with magic." (personal communication)).

I began receiving their *Elf Magic Mail* (see our two books of that title), as they called them, from then on. Each week three printed letters with graphics would arrive in an envelope illuminating various aspects of elfin life and philosophy. At first, I had a difficult time understanding them. They seemed to make sense and no sense at the same time. One evening after receiving them for several months I finally understood them. It was as though I had been trying to read them in English when they were actually written in Elven, a parallel language that looked like English but had different meanings or "thought emotes" (Silver Elves, 2014) for many of the words. What I realized was that all that time I had been reading the text literally without reading between the lines where the real message lay concealed.

Not long after that I was invited to visit them at their home in Aurora. It would turn out to be a most enlightening encounter.

All My Life

It seemed to me at the time that I had been awaiting almost my entire life for something to happen. Not just anything to happen, but a special set of circumstances or an event that would signal the moment had come. I would have been unable to tell you at that time what exactly those circumstances were. Had I been able to do so it would have made no difference, for the circumstances could not occur upon request. They could not occur because I asked someone to fulfill that need. They had to happen spontaneously. And yet, even if I wanted to do so, I could not have told someone what to do to fulfill that need. I did not know. I simply felt it deep within me, carried it around for years... waiting... waiting for something that it seemed would never come. It was as though there was a program hidden in my unconscious that would only be released or enacted if these particular circumstances occurred. I was like someone hypnotized, waiting for the trigger word to make them behave in a particular way (note that this is the theme of a number of spy movies, only my program was Cosmic), I awaited a set of circumstances that would unleash a torrent within me.

One evening, sitting between two beautiful, loving and affectionate elf sisters, daughters of the Elf Queen, I found myself overwhelmed by emotion. Tears spilled from my eyes. My typical callous and cynical skepticism fled, leaving me with only my naked heart and feelings. I knew in that moment that I was an elf and that I had been awaiting all my life for my kindred to come and find me and finally they had. This is not a feeling peculiar to me. Numerous elves, including our sister Syleniel (personal communication) who help found the Elenari elves, feel particularly moved when listening to Peter Gabriel's song *Solsbury Hill* that has this as a theme.

I Ching

It was at that moment that we turned to the I Ching, which is how the sisters looked at every situation, and used the sticks for deriving an oracle. The I Ching is an ancient Chinese form of divination, arrived at by a process of dividing sticks or throwing coins. It is over four thousands years old (although among the elves it is said it is at least eight thousand) and was used by Jung in his exploration to develop the idea of synchronicity. I had done the I Ching previously a few times but didn't really know how to use it. The EQD used the Ching at least daily and were masters in its use. Some 20 years later, when Silver Flame and I became active participants in their Sorcery Group, they would also declare me to be a Ching Master. Thus I could say that I not only have a Masters degree in Speech Communications and Depth Psychology, but also, in keeping with my personal myth, in Divinatory Studies.

The Ching I received that evening, *Revolution* hexagram number 49 (Wilhelm, 1967; Reifler, 1974) struck me as being so accurate in describing the current state of my psyché that it added tremendously to the sense of destiny that was already flooding through me. This was particularly true since, although I have found the Wilhelm/Baynes translation to be the best, it was the Reifler translation that spoke that evening so profoundly to my experience, telling me I was in the midst of changing my spiritual philosophy. (I was at that time an active member of Divine Light Mission, a meditation society, and had been previously initiated in and practiced the meditation techniques taught by the Ananda Marga group and the Transcendental Meditation folks.) I have been using the I Ching daily ever since. (Also see our book an *Elven Book of Changes*, 2012a.)

However, although I had been an active member of meditation groups and had gradually improved my ability to meditate (at first sitting still for more than five minutes was pure torture) I had still felt something was missing from my life. That changed when I found the Elf Queen's Daughters. In fact, I had a friend in that period of my life, a young, beautiful woman who I would hang out with from time to time. Just after I awakened to my elven nature, we took a walk around the lake at Southern Illinois University, and I told her of this new development in my life. She listened and then smiled at me and revealed that she had never felt that Divine Light Mission was quite right for me and that she felt certain that being an elf was my true path. This was a profound confirmation to me.

We Burnt Our Names In Flame

In the original formulation of this book in the form of my thesis I had written that "We had a ritual among the EQD where we would write our names on a piece of paper, throw it in a fire and taking the ash from the fire anoint our foreheads and swear to return lifetime after lifetime until all our kindred that been found and awakened." In truth, some of the *Elf Magic Mail* spoke of burning our names and at a Yule gathering an elven sister and I created an impromptu ceremony of burning our names as described. I only shortened the story to make it simpler for my Thesis, however, this led a scholar in Denmark who read my thesis for his Doctoral Dissertation to mistakenly assume we had such rituals in the EQD, which wasn't the case. In all the years I've known the sisters of the EQD, as witches, elves and sorcerers, they never did anything that could be described as ritual or ceremony, unless one considers doing the I Ching frequently as ritual. But even then we would talk and chat among ours'elves as we'd pass the sticks around. In fact, some of the letters of the *Elf Magic Mail* (Silver Elves, 2014) spoke very clearly about a lack of ceremony or ritual among the elven sisterhood.

We might mention, however, that while the Elf Queen's Daughters and we Silver Elves are not inclined toward ritual (repetitive magics), we Silver Elves have experimented with traditional Western Ceremonial Magick, as we in fact experiment with nearly every magic system we encounter, and there is certainly nothing wrong with elves having or doing rituals if that is their desire. We have, in fact, written two books (Silver Elves, vol. 1 2012e; vol. 2 2012f) on ritual and ceremonial magick giving examples and suggestions for those who wish to create their own ceremonies as well as offering some of our thoughts and ideas concerning ceremonial magick.

Alas, while this sister and I made this vow quite sincerely, the reality was that the EQD was soon gone. After a year, the Aurora elves moved west, and slowly people fell away. Those who had been writing the *Elf Magic Mail* (Silver Elves, 2014) stopped doing so, and while they continued on the occult path they abandoned interacting with the world as elves. One sister died in a motorcycle accident, which was considered a very bad omen, and the others, including the one who had taken the vow with me, simply fell back into the world. However, I could not forget. I had sworn a vow and I intended to keep it.

Unfortunately, I didn't feel very powerful as an elf, but perhaps that wasn't what was needed. The Elf Queen's Daughters had been potent witches. They were hot. Their magic was real and powerful, and they knew it and used it freely. Alas, like many others through the ages the temptation to slip into the dark side of manipulation was too much for them, and like many, many before, the spirits brought them down, scattering them to the four winds. This left me, an elf who had little in the way of power but who had a great deal in perseverance born of the illuminated vision and experience, to carry on. I had been stirred to the depths of my soul and simply could not give up.

A Sign

With the disappearance of the Elf Magic Mail (I still received personal letters from the sisters) and the dispersion of the elves, I felt terribly alone. Suddenly it seemed that I was one of the very few still upon this path, and none of those who remained lived anywhere near me. I continued on, but doubt became more and more prominent in my heart and mind.

After nearly a year of this, I despaired. Was I just kidding mys'elf sticking to a path that nearly everyone else had abandoned? Was I a fool to believe in magic at all when nearly everyone else thought it was a ridiculous notion?

I decided to find out. I asked the spirits for a sign, a sign that would tell me that this was indeed the right path for me. A sign that would, by its very nature, confirm the reality of the magic.

At first nothing happened. I went about my life alert to the possibility of a message from the spirit world, but for weeks nothing occurred except one wee thing. I came across a sign in the local natural foods store, written on a three by five card, announcing a party to be held at a place called Rivendell, obviously named after the elfin village in Tolkien's *Lord of the Rings*. However, the card gave no address or phone number, and when I inquired of the people who worked at the store, they had never heard of the place. I was back to square one, and I soon forgot about Rivendell.

I was in the habit at that time of drawing one of the Sabian Symbols from Dane Rudhyar's *Astrological Mandala* (1973) each day, which contained an archetypal interpretation for 360 symbols, one for each degree of the Zodiac, as an oracle. One day I received a symbol that spoke of receiving a sign, and I knew that my request was to be answered that day, one way or another. (Also see our book *The Elven Book of Dreams*, 2012b.)

As it happened, a couple I knew had invited me to go with them to some party to be held in the country side, and I spent the entire time on the drive there, looking for the sign. Alas, nothing appeared. And as it turned out, it was a typical party with a keg of beer and a bunch of strangers standing about talking. I have never cared for beer and, being an introvert, was none too adept at striking up conversations with strangers. So I did what I so often did at parties. I walked into the nearby forest to speak to the trees. I was still looking for that sign, something, anything that would affirm or deny my chosen path.

But nothing happened. I found nothing unusual on the ground. Encountered no deer or bird or anything that might in the least way be construed to be an answer to my request. Finally, frustrated and coming to the conclusion that the lack of a sign was my answer, I returned to the party to wait it out until my friends decided to go home.

As I was standing around, I noticed an older man who I was told was the owner of the property. To be polite I introduced mys'elf, and he, in turn, told me his name but added, "But my friends call me Elrond [the name of an elf character in the Lord of the Rings], because I named this place Rivendell."

This was indeed my sign. It came the day the oracle said it would come. And it was utterly unambiguous in its reply. The Elfin Path was clearly my own.

The Birth Of A Star Queen

I felt horribly inadequate to carry on the work of awakening and nurturing elves lost in the modern world, but having sworn to do so I felt I had no alternative. My personal sense of integrity and honor simply wouldn't let me give up and I just couldn't embrace a life in the mundane world from which I'd always felt alienated and toward which I felt no affinity. Yet, though I wished to continue on my elven path, I especially felt inadequate to continue the labor of giving birth to the *Elf Magic*

73

Mail (Silver Elves, 2014a 2014b), which had so deeply impressed and inspired me and keep me going for several years.

In the meantime, many things had happened. I had a friend who had known the original two founders of the EQD years before its inception and had, in fact, been there that very night that they had channeled a spirit's message on the Ouija board (a board with the alphabet and the numbers 1 to 10 upon it used for channeling messages, and typically sold as a game in children's toy stores) instructing them to established the Elf Queen's Daughters. We began doing magic together, and among the many results of those workings was the birth of a daughter we named Elantari (which means Star Queen) Emerald Love.

Six months later, we went to live with the Tookes, which is what the founders of the Elf Queen's Daughters now called thems'elves, with whom I had continued a correspondence despite the cessation of the *Elf Magic Mail*. They had become hobbits, they said, and that was all right with us. They indicated that they felt that calling thems'elves elves had been a bit arrogant and calling thems'elves hobbits was a bit more modest (personal communication). As I said previously, they had been quite powerful as elven witches but had perhaps reveled in that power too much. This seemed to confirm this notion.

However, after a little over a month of being with them we discovered to our dismay that they found children a terrible inconvenience and there was simply no way I was going to raise my daughter among them. (Note that the birth of a grandson and granddaughter in their family years later significantly altered their attitude toward having children about.) Plus, I had no intention of giving up my elven path. They may have embraced being hobbits and half-elven, for they still sang the songs of praise to Elbereth (Tolkien, 1979b), and while I was glad enough to be a hobbit among them, in my heart I continued to be an elf. I like hobbits but did not resonant with that persona.

I might point out that in the intervening years, from 1978 when we lived with them to the mid 1990's when we joined and participated in their Sorcery Group, they still called thems'elves hobbits, yet still would spontaneously sing the songs for the Elf Goddess Elbereth (Tolkien, 1979b). But they had also, in fact, come to look ever more like hobbits. Except for our sister Loriel who retained her slimmer elven look, but then even back in 1978 they would tease her about still wishing to be an elfin faerie princess, which to our eyes she will ever be. This is to say that as you live your myth, you become your myth. Magic is a process of doing and becoming. What you do, the way you live, is what you are, and formulates what you become.

The Silver Flame

As it happened, some months before we left Carbondale for California where the Tookes lived, I had met a young woman at my workplace. She was almost exactly my age. She was merely passing through town with her boyfriend on a road trip and they were just working for a while to make enough money to travel on. She would not work where I worked for more than a week, yet despite that, I kept running into her afterwards here and there by coincidence, or synchronicity, around town and we became friends. She had a Master's degree, as I did, and was in so many ways, very much like me. There was an instantaneous rapport between us. She was one of those people one meets that one recognizes from previous lifetimes.

We invited her and her boyfriend to dinner and we showed them the magic baby room where I had, for nearly a year, been doing magic to bless, protect and attract the elven babies who would be coming into the world. Two days later, she was pregnant, and within the month returned with her boyfriend to Gainesville, Fl. from whence they'd come. (A longer tale of the magic baby room and the magic we did there can be found in an article we wrote that was published in Circle Network News.)

Tree's Dream

In 1979, I moved with my family to Gainesville, Fl. to be near this woman, to whom I gifted the elven name, Silver Flame (who, eight years later and three thousand miles further west, would become my mate and has been my constant companion for the last 27+ years). We settled in Gainesville in an apartment near her, but in time, we found a house, a bit out in the country, to share with a lady I had met through work. Her name was Tree.

Now Tree knew we were elves, because, well, we tell everyone who gets to know us even a little bit that we are elves, but we never spoke to her of the Elf Queen's Daughters, and she knew nothing of the *Elf Magic Mail*, which I so longed to continue but still felt utterly inadequate to do.

One morning, about a month or so after we had moved in, she came to me perplexed. She told me she had a dream. She said, that she had no idea what the dream meant, but she had been told in the dream that it was a message for me. Tree had dreamt that she was walking in the woods when she had come upon three women (there were, at that time, three Tookes, all formally of the Elf Queen's Daughters, all women) sitting beneath a tree holding a golden book. Then they had gotten up and left the book lying at the base of the tree. When she approached the tree and picked up the book the tree said to her, "Tell Zardoa, this is now his."

Tree asked me if the dream made any sense to me, for it was a total blank for her. I told her that indeed the dream meant very much to me, although I never explained how or why, but merely thanked her profusely for having delivered the message.

It was indeed clear to me what the dream had meant. The spirits of the forest had sent me a message; I had been empowered to write the letters that I now called the *Magical Elven Love Letters*. I had inherited a Dharma, which is to say a spiritual mission and responsibility, and I accepted it gladly. Although at first I still felt inadequate to the task, often reading old letters from the EQD to inspire me, I now felt without a doubt that this was the path I was to take. I soon started creating *The Magical Elven Love Letters*, and sending them out by snail mail, and later by email. They have been published into three books, vols. 1, 2 (2007-2011b) and 3 (2012c). The first being (Silver Elves, 2001b) a 300 page collection of these writings.

The Living Myth

Over thirty years ago, I went with some friends to visit a person who turned out to be the ex-husband of one of them. When I met the man, he told me that he had heard so much about me from so many different sources over such a long period that he considered me a living myth. "Not a legend," he said, "But a Myth."

About fifteen years later and about 1,500 miles further west, I was walking around the Sebastopol Flea Market where I had been reading tarot every weekend for a dollar a reading, when one of my customers came up to me and informed me that she had told a friend of hers in Sacramento (over a 100 miles further east) about me, and her friend had already heard of me from someone else. She said, "You're like a living myth." I knew at that moment that something was in process, and I thought to mys'elf if anyone ever says that to me again (the law of three in magic) then the Mythos would be born, and I would have had the great privilege of being the living person from whence the myth evolved. It would, of course, separate from

77

me, spin off in the world and live its own mythological life. I would have had the honor, in that case, of being the actuality from which it had originated, as the Picts evolved into the mythos of the Pixies (Gardner, 2003) and someone, probably one of the Sami people, a Laplander, was the source of the myth of Santa Claus.

About fifteen years later, thirty years after the first incident, just after the movie the *Fellowship of the Ring* had come out and just after my wife Silver Flame and I had published our *Book of Elven Runes* (Silver Elves, 2001a), Silver Flame was talking to me about our book and our elven life and said, "You know what we are? We're like living myths." Now, because this was Silver Flame and because I had told her my living myth anecdotes, even though it had been over ten years since I'd mentioned them, I was compelled to regard her utterance of this statement as questionable confirmation, since it had not come from an independent and spontaneous source. Clearly, she could have been unconsciously bringing out what she had heard previously but forgotten. However, her statement put me on alert, and I became open to the possibility that the confirming sign might soon come. Something from an independent source that would proclaim, this is indeed, the third sign.

It was not long in coming. That afternoon we went grocery shopping and, while doing so, encountered a fellow that we had known but briefly, having met him while attending our third screening of the *Fellowship of the Ring*. He had been let in to the theatre free because he had already seen the movie so many times that they told him he was a frequent flyer. We showed him our new book, and upon examining it, and buying it, he commented, "You know what you are doing here? You're creating your own mythology. You're like a living myth in the world." That was clearly and irrefutably the third sign.

As a sideline, our apologies to Christine Wicker, the author of *Not In Kansas Anymore* (2005). She had interviewed us for that book and we had told her the above story that she wanted to include in that book but we asked her not to do so (a request which she honored) because we felt at the time it seemed a bit immodest to mention it, even though it is a true story. However, we put it in this book because it is utterly germane to our thesis and the subject of this work.

Grandchild of the Spirits

According to Narby (1998) the South American shamans say that tobacco is the grandchild of the spirits. When I first read that in his book I decided to include tobacco, which I knew Native North Americans also used as offerings to the spirit world, in my shamanic practices. However, Narby suggested that the carcinogenic cigarettes that are popular in the normal culture, might poison the spirits, and therefore I began looking for tobacco that would not include additives. I settled upon a simple pack of cigars, which are frequently used by Central American shamans.

About a couple of weeks after making my first offering to the spirits of tobacco smoke, I went to visit a friend who lives in the hills around Occidental, Ca. To get to his house, you must pass another that shares the same driveway. As I was walking up the drive a young girl called out to me from her open kitchen window, "Hey, would you like some plants?"

"What kind of plants?" I asked.

"Tobacco," she replied, "I have a whole bunch of them that were brought up from Guatemala, and I just don't need this many."

To me, this was a sign from the spirits that they were pleased with my offerings, and wanted me to continue, since, after all, they were now providing the tobacco. I accepted the plants and began growing them, rolling them into cigars and offering them to the spirits in many of my magic workings, as we will see as this study continues.

(In 2008, however, we moved to Hawaii and I couldn't take my plants with me, so I've gone back to using cigars, the latest batch I bought from a native tribe woman from Myramar, when the spirits took us to Northern Thailand.)

Magic

The nature of the mythology of the elves cannot be considered properly without addressing the idea of Magic, for magic is integral to fairy tales and the elven myths and is central to Elven Culture. However, magic is a very loaded word that elicits a variety of responses, similar to the responses one receives to declaring one is an elf.

Most people of scientific disposition regard magic as irrational and airy-fairy (Mahrer, 2001) (I love that term) which, in fact, is the same way, curiously, that they often regard qualitative research such as this study. Others regard magic with a kind of secret dread and sometimes, the individuals of the first type are also of the second, believing magic to be irrational and unscientific and at the same time holding that secret dread just in case it is real. (Rather like many people's reactions to ghosts; they don't believe, but just in case. Or how most people seem to view death, god and the afterlife. They don't really believe there is anything beyond death but they pretend they do.)

Depth Psychology, which is much more open than most disciplines to examining mystical or occult phenomena as related to the psyché, generally approaches magic indirectly. There are numerous books which relate Shamanism and psychology, ritual and psychology, but almost none speak of magic, of which shamanism is one method. Some of the most notable of these texts are *Shamanism and the Psychology of C.G. Jung* (Ryan, 2002), *The Shaman's Body* (Mindell, 1993) and *The Shaman's Doorway* (Larsen, 1988).

While psychology has endeavored to understand shamanism and thus magic from a psychological point of view, it has done little to understand it from the point of view of the magician or shaman, and that perspective is vital to an understanding of my personal myth. For I am a magician, an elven enchanter. What follows will be an attempt to define magic and, in as much as possible, to relate it to various schools of psychology. For magic and psychology do indeed have much in common. The difference is that magic continues into that place that psychology often fears to tread.

If the Elves had our way,

we'd be friends with everyone.

That some folk choose not to be our friends

is eternally a mystery to us,

for they do not realize

the wonders they are missing out on.

Shakespeare wrote that
all the world is a play
and all of us players
and in that he was surely fey touched,
for this is the elfin view of reality:
"All is as we make it,
rather than fixed eternally beforehand."
—Ancient elfin knowledge

CHAPTER 4:

WHAT IS MAGIC?

> *"Fairies are generally associated with the ability to perform magic of one sort or another... Their magic was essentially geared to outstanding gifts of perception, along with their ability to access the wisdom of Elphame."* (Gardner, 2000, p. 110)

In This Chapter

It is no small task to try to encompass magical theory into one small chapter. However,

I shall attempt to do so. Because this is a psychological thesis, and, because I assume many readers will come to it from an interest in, and perhaps, background of, psychology, I will endeavor to connect magical theory with psychological theory, so that the reader will have a basis for entering, what is for most, an alien world.

I will also, in this chapter, distinguish Elfin magic from the traditional view of Western magic, and demonstrate how Elfin magic is similar, indeed, nearly identical to the psychological view of Depth Psychology.

Elves do not strive to be better than others

but to be ever better ourselves.

So What is Magic?

Magic in a very simple way is an attempt to control those aspects of life that seem to be beyond our control. You can, for instance, apply for a job and be utterly qualified for the position but what makes it likely that you will be chosen over the dozen to hundred other applicants? This is the province of magic. And magic is fundamental to this thesis because within my personal myth magic is very real, vital and valid. Thus, to understand my personal myth it is important to understand what I actually mean by magic.

Sir James Frazer (1951/1922) tells us that:

Wherever ... magic occurs in its pure unadulterated form, it is assumed that in nature one event follows another necessarily and invariably without the intervention of any spiritual or personal agency.

Thus the fundamental conception is identical with that of modern science; underlying the whole system is a faith, implicit but real and firm, in the order and uniformity of nature. (p. 56).

Frazer (1951/1922) is of the opinion that while the magician's understanding of the basic uniformity of nature is accurate, the shaman, in his primitive mind, fails in making the proper associations as to what causes what. Much as Piaget (1950) points out the erroneous causal links that children often make between things when they are in the developmental stage in which "magical thinking" is prominent. Because of this failure, aboriginal man in time abandoned magic and accepted religion (Frazer, 1951/1922) and Frazer concluded that magic had the right idea of cause and effect, but was in practice, faulty, superstitious, and erroneous, and thus invalidly attributing causes to acts that, in fact, had no real connection to the desired effect. The aboriginal magician, in other words, mistook coincidence with cause, and from that Frazer concluded that magic is superstition.

Whereas, I conclude that while aboriginal magicians were at times inaccurate in their causal associations, the basic principles of magic could still be valid. We do not abandon the scientific method simply because so many of its theories and hypotheses have proven to be invalid in the course of time and discovery. We need not abandon magic because its spells are not always effective.

Aleister Crowley (1976/1929), one of the most notorious magicians of the twentieth century and a major theorist of magic in modern times, wrote that, "Magic is the Science and Art of causing Change to occur in conformity with Will." (p. XII). Like Frazer, he saw magic as being basically (but not absolutely) scientific in its principles. This approach is not very different, in my view, from Behaviorism, where one applies the principles of science, positive reinforcement, etc., to affect change in the behavior of animals and humans (Fadiman, Frager, 1974).

Crowley (1976/1929) also wrote that "Every intentional act is a Magical Act." (p. XIII). Yet are we to believe that if I intend to turn on the light and I go and do it, that that is an act of magic? If we are to go strictly by that definition we would have to assume so. Yet, what individual, even those who don't believe in the efficacy of magic, would define magic in such a materialistic way?

I believe, and I think common belief would hold, that magic, while it may not involve the intervention of personal or spiritual agencies (by which is meant praying to, supplicating or begging Gods for help, unlike Western Ceremonial Magick where the magician stands as God of his own circle and commands obedience from lesser, although powerful, spirits) indicates the power of psychic force. What makes magic *magic* is that there is no discernible link between the magician's act of magic and the result of the magic, except for his magical action, which sets in motion psychic, which is to say invisible, forces or powers of Nature.

As an example, let's say I'm a single fellow desirous of meeting an eligible lady. I do some magic for that purpose, and within a week or so I happen to encounter just such a lady, as if by accident. Now, your scientific sort will argue that this is just a coincidence and that there is no reliable link between my act of magic and my encounter with the lady. And I would have to agree with them. There is no discernible link between the two. That's why it's called magic. At the same time, there's no denying that the one followed in due time after the other. The scientific mind would demand proof that the act of magic caused the lady to appear. The magician is content that his or her act was followed by the desired result. Magicians are, for the most part, less interested in proving the validity of magic than in reaping the rewards of its use.

Now, the empirical scientist will counter that we have a case of false reasoning, just as children in the *magical thinking stage* see links between things that are not actually connected, I, as the magician, they would say, have made the same error. To test the magic, according to their point of view, I would have to repeat the experiment, noting if every time I did my magical act, I met an eligible lady. Otherwise, we'd have to conclude that there was indeed no casual connection between the two. Science is seeking to discover absolute connections and links of cause; magic seeks to heighten and accentuate probability and possibility.

Ars Magica

But what if magic is not so much a science but an art, which depends on the power of aesthetics and the creative imagination as well as skill to create an effect, rather than direct causality? Crowley (1976/1929), remember, defined magic as an art and a science. And Frazer (1951/1922) tells us that for the "primitive" (p. 13) magician whose logic was implicit rather than explicit, "... magic is always an art, never a science; the very idea of science is lacking in his undeveloped mind." (p. 13). In other words, it was Frazer who saw early magic as a failed attempt at science, which was never the magician's view at all. The attempt to make magic like science is the attempt to take most of the magic out of magic.

Magical Formulas

Let's take, for example, the process of making movies. I could study the greatest movies ever made and learn all the techniques for making great movies and follow them exactly. Does that guarantee that I will make a great movie? Certainly, good technique is important and understanding the principles upon which great movies are made can be significant. Those comprise the scientific part of movie making.

However, there is also an artistic part of movie making (or should be) and without it, without the originality and creativity, the best techniques and formulas fall flat. So, too, when magicians follow formulas like chemists and expect to get the same results over and over again, they often fail. Magic is not merely a science, not even primarily a science, but an art. Without that creative spark, without that originality, magic has no life.

Maturity Of The Magician

A chemist, if he puts together the correct chemicals in the proper measure, order, mode, etc., will inevitably arrive at the same result. For him personal maturity or development is of little consequence in his ability to produce results. However, the magician's powers, which is to say his/her chances of success, are very affected by his/her personal being and maturity (Bardon, 1975).

For the magician is an artist, and he must have talent and a passion to fulfill it. If I were to have to choose between seeing an original and creative movie without technical skill or polish that was exciting to watch, or a movie that was technically marvelous but without a sense of soul or excitement, I would naturally choose the first. However, if I were to have my own way, I would have the movie be both exciting and technically well made. The magician and the artist are empowered by skill. That is where magic becomes science, but it must never be forgotten that it is an Art, first and forever foremost. This is particularly true of Elfish magic for the aim of Elvish magic is ever beauty and art, rather than science. In many ways, one might say that the purpose of Elfin magic is not so much to change the world, as make it more mysterious and beautiful. Of course, one might point out that making the world more beautiful is changing the world, and we elves surely would not disagree.

Tolkien (1977a) wrote, "Faerie itself may perhaps most nearly be translated by Magic — but it is a magic of a peculiar mood and power, at the furthest pole from the vulgar devices of the laborious, scientific, magician." (p. 17).

Starhawk

Starhawk (1989/1979) wrote that "Magic was the art of changing consciousness at will" (p. 7). She gives credit for this definition to Dion Fortune, a contemporary of Crowley, the great modern theorist of magic, but says she can not remember exactly where she read it and thus is unable to properly credit it (Starhawk, personal communication) (In our own research we never found this statement in Fortune's writings, although we've read quite of bit of it, but found this definition in W. E. Butler's book *The Magician: His Training and Work*, (1959); however, since Butler was a student of Fortune's he may very well have received it from her).

Here, ever so slightly we have shifted our definition. Is magic the art of changing one's mind and attitude and perhaps others' attitudes as well? Here we have magic as Cognitive Psychology, which emphasizes the transformative power of positive thinking and attitudes for improving our life (Fadiman, Frager, 1974). I in no way deny the tremendous, life-transforming power of altering one's thoughts, beliefs, attitudes, etc. A person who has the ability to change people's mind could change the world. Look at the effect the ideas of Jesus, Buddha and Mohamed have had upon millions of people over thousands of years.

In this view, magic functions in the realm of the psyché, but primarily in the conscious aspect of the psyché. However, I would suggest that magic does not function exclusively nor even primarily in the conscious mind. Magic, by its very nature, and particularly Elfin magic, functions in the realm of the invisible unconscious as well. Indeed, I might very well say that magic results from an active and intentional communication between the two, between the conscious and unconscious. True magic stems from the integration of the magician's psyché and an evocation of the mythic and imaginal aspects arising from the unconscious.

As Above/So Below

We must remember that the most aboriginal, and thus in a sense, elfin (Evans-Wentz, 1966) shaman/magicians were animists. Everything was alive in their world. And those things

89

that were not organically alive, such as swords, had the potential to house life. This is why the Japanese Samurai believed his sword had a spirit and soul (Suino,1994) and why King Arthur and Aragorn (the hero of the Lord of the Rings) had swords with names (Ratti, Westbrook,1973).

In a magical world, everything is alive and everything is connected to everything else. However, the vast majority of those interconnections are invisible to the eyes of everyone but the wise and knowing. Frazer (1951/1922) said that for the primitive magician there were two essential types of magic. The first is Sympathetic magic in which like affects like. And the second is Contagious magic in which any two things that were ever connected still have a connection of experience and thus can still affect each other.

The morphic resonance, which Rupert Sheldrake (1995) posits as existing throughout nature, and that Fienstien (1998) has extended to the psyché and the basic theories of field theory, are, and always have been, basic principles of magical thought throughout the ages. This is similar to Jung's idea of the collective unconscious (Stein, 1998), which is inherited instinctual knowledge shared by particular groups, races and humanity at large. However, here is posited a collective unconscious that exists not only in individuals but is interconnected between individuals. Everything in the universe is connected and the magician can thus accomplish anything if he/she understands the proper lines of force or connection (Crowley, 1976).

Magic Made Simple

Let's return to our simplest definition of magic. Magic is an intentional act. We have added to that, the idea that it is applied or accomplished through forces that are for the most part

90

invisible, for the purpose of creating a particular effect or result. However, there is another form of magic and that is magic that is not the result of anything we have done intentionally but which simply happens, as the bumper sticker proclaims: Magic Happens. Magic as a form of luck or magic as a result of good karma. Let's say that you had a rich uncle that you never knew existed who leaves you a fortune. Now, you may have done no magic to make this happen, but who upon receiving a check for millions of dollars wouldn't feel that some great magic had occurred? This brings us to Elfin magic and how it differs from "the vulgar devices of the laborious, scientific, magician." (Tolkien, 1977a, p. 17). Elfin magic, as Tolkien points out to us, is not the magic of science and direct causality, but a magic born of the imaginal and the aesthetic. It is the difference between combining chemicals that you know will cause a powerful explosion when ignited and creating a beautiful painting that will ignite a powerful reaction in many, perhaps most of its viewers. Remember, enchantment describes both the act of magic and its result.

Ancient Chinese Elves

The I Ching (Wilhelm, 1967), which was created by the ancient Taoist magicians and alchemists that the elves consider to be our ancestors in spirit if not in genetics, says, "When the quiet power of a man's own character is at work, the effects produced are right. All those who are receptive to the vibrations of such a spirit will then be influenced. Influence over others should not express itself as a conscious and willed effort to manipulate them. Through practicing such conscious incitement, one becomes wrought up and is exhausted by the eternal stress and strain. Moreover, the effects produced are then limited to those on whom one's thoughts are consciously fixed." (p. 124-5).

91

For the elves, like our ancestors who created the I Ching, the power of magic comes not from trying to manipulate every little thing but from developing ours'elves to the point where the magic just happens. This brings us to one of Jung's (1962) favorite stories, one that Wilhelm told him of his experience watching a Taoist rainmaker in China. Wilhelm was in a village where it had not rained in ages and in desperation they sent to another region for a rainmaker. The rainmaker came, and asked for a hut on the edge of the village, where he secluded himself for days until it rained. When Wilhelm asked him how he made it rain, the rainmaker told him that when he came to the village everyone was out of tune with the Tao, which made him out of tune as well. Thus, he spent days meditating until he brought himself in harmony with the Tao, and when he had accomplished that, the rain, naturally, fell.

So it is with Elfin magic. By becoming in tune with the Tao, with Nature, within ours'elves, by becoming as Jung called it Individuating, life flows to us naturally. Everything becomes as it is meant to be.

Crowley (1976, p. xix) writes, "Every individual is essentially sufficient to himself. But he is unsatisfactory to himself until he has established himself in his right relation with the Universe." While the world is vast and beyond our immediate control, we optimize our success therein by bringing ours'elves into harmony within ours'elves and thereby find our true place in the universe in which all that happens, happens for a purpose and that purpose is the fulfillment of our individual and collective being.

It is only by becoming in tune with our entire being, which is achieved by means of individuating... that is becoming and accepting who we truly are, that true Elfin magic becomes possible. We can never hope to fulfill Elvish magics when we are not in tune with our own natures. By individuating, by becoming complete beings, we open the doorway to the entirety of ours'elves. And in so doing we begin the journey into Elfin, that realm where all things have meaning and synchronicities are an everyday occurrence.

Elf Luck

To the elves, magic and luck are essentially the same thing. By developing our inner natures, we attract luck to us. We do not seek to compel the world to be as we think best, unceasingly seeking to manipulate every little thing as so many do; but rather, do our upmost to be the best we can be and therefore allow and encourage the best to flow to us.

Ritual

Ritual as conceived by the wiccans/witches is a form of worship (Starhawk, 1989,1979). Ritual for magicians is a formula for calling spirits or setting in motion forces that will enact their will. The traditional magicians use words of power (Crowley, 1976: Bardon, 1975) and the evocation of "barbarous names" to compel spirits to do their bidding. However, the elves are not inclined to try to force anyone to do anything. For us, the ritual or magical act is a symbolic communication to the spirit world telling the spirits what we desire.

The traditional magician seals himself within the magic circle to protect him from harm. For often those he summons are demons or elementals of great power who are looking for the slightest loophole by which they may thwart the magician's directives (Crowley, 1976) just as workers who are employed by a boss they hate secretly do things to undermine him. (At military school, we loved to see how far we could bend the rules without getting in trouble for breaking them.) We elves on the other hand, do our best to avoid demons. The spirits with whom we interact are, for the most part, seen as relatives. We do not compel them but rather, in many cases, pay them with energy, just as one would pay a plumber, to do as one wishes.

Enchantment

Tolkien (1977a) wrote: "...the more potent and specially elvish craft I will... call Enchantment" (p. 54). For we elves are enchanters. We fulfill our wishes not through coercion or force but by creating wonder and joy. The I Ching (Wilhelm, 1967) states, "Under certain conditions, intimidation without gentleness may achieve something momentarily, but not for all time. When, on the other hand, the hearts of men are won by friendliness, they are led to take all hardships upon themselves willingly, and if need be will not shun death itself, so great is the power of joy over men." (p. 224) Such is the power of enchantment. Such is the magic of the elves. Enchantment, I will further define then as magic that achieves its results through attraction rather than compulsion.

Enchantment is not direct cause and effect, like traditional magic, but rather creation of an atmosphere that heightens the possibility of the desired result. It is more in tune with the doing by not doing of Zen and Taoism.

Religion

As we said previously, and as Frazer (1951/1922) pointed out, the aboriginal (elven) magician "supplicates no higher power: he sues the favor of no fickle and wayward being: he abases himself before no awful deity." (p. 56). The earliest societies, according to Frazer had no religion at all, they were pre-religious. And that is true of this elf as well, I follow no religion.

Yet, does that mean I am agnostic or atheist? By no means. I believe in all the gods and goddesses. Just as I believe in Santa Claus, Peter Pan and the Tooth Fairy. I really do. I'm not being facetious. But while I give them due respect, I worship none of them. Nor do I believe in a God outside of creation. Rather, I believe in a Divine essence which lives in potential in all things and which we as individuals have come into the world to make manifest within our own beings. (Note that we elves often view the Divine, the miraculous and magic as being essentially the same thing.)

However, while these elves do not follow a religion, it doesn't mean that other elves don't or shouldn't. As we said previously, every elf has a right, and responsibility really, to decide for hir (his/her) own s'elf what spiritual path they wish to follow and how they will follow it. For instance, one elf sister of ours, Calantirniel, has taken Tolkien's (1977b) writings and created Tië Eldaliéva, an elven spiritual path based on his works (Carding, 2012).

Activism

Since Elfin magic is primarily dependent upon the maturity and development of the individual, the question arises as to its place in interacting with the world as it exists. Does the Elfin magician have any responsibility to try to affect social change, as is the case of the wiccan magic of Starhawk (1982), which is geared very strongly toward social activism?

The answer would depend, as it so often does with elves, upon the individual. Each elf, acting as a free spirit, must decide for thems'elves what their duty is. The I Ching (Wilhelm, 1967) says there are two basic paths a person can take in life, that of the hero and that of the sage. The hero goes forth in the world with an intent to make it better, while the sage has the responsibility to lead an exemplary life. The sage goes out and meets the future, so to speak, by living in such ways that he/she feels would make the world better if others chose to live that way as well. The sage lives ahead of his or her time. Confucius would be an example of the first way, Lao Tzu, the founder of Taoism, of the second.

The choice of which of these two paths to follow is left to the individual and the Ching says, "There is no general law to say which of the two is the right way. Each one in this situation must make a free choice according to the inner law of his [her] being. If the individual acts consistently and is true to himself, he will find the way that is appropriate for him." (p. 9).

Choosing the way of the hero, however, does not free one from the obligation to develop ones'elf, nor does choosing the way of the sage free one from any responsibility in the world.

Responsibility

The problem with being a magician is you have to accept responsibility for everything you do and in the course of time, everything that happens to you. You can no longer whine that life just wasn't fair. You can no longer blame God because things went wrong. If you are truly on the path of magic you know that ultimately, whatever happens is your responsibility, and worse yet, possibly, your fault, either because you did the magic incorrectly or because your will was thwarted by the more potent incantations of other sorcerers (Frazer, 1951/1922). You might ask, how is it my responsibility that others are more powerful than I? And the answer is that the magician is responsible for everything he/she does, doesn't do and is too weak to do effectively. If my powers are not potent enough, whose responsibility is that? Mine, always mine. It is my responsibility to make my life what I wish it to be. It is my responsibility to make mys'elf strong enough to fulfill that wish. To be a magician is to accept responsibility for everything I do, and for everything that happens to me.

(For more extended writings about Elven magic and philosophy, see our books *Through the Mists of Faerie: A Magical Guide to the Wisdom Teachings of the Ancient Elven* (2012d) and *The Elven Way: The Magical Path of the Shining Ones* (2013a).)

Family

Fortunately, elves are never alone, even when we find ours'elves without a friend in the material world. For elves know thems'elves to be a part of a family, a family of spirits, and in a family no one is ever solely responsible. We are all responsible for ours'elves; it is true. However, we are also, all responsible for each other. My wishes are not for mys'elf alone, but for my kindred as well. What benefits me; benefits them and vice versa. Ken Eagle Feather (1995) writes that he asked Florida Donner, one of the members of Carlos Castaneda's sorcery group, what binds a magical team together and she replied "Affection." It is love that encourages us to take on responsibility for our others. It is mutual affection. This is surely what has bound elves together through the ages, affection for each other and an unending affection for all things Faerie.

While the traditional western magician stands alone as god in the center of his magic circle/universe (Bardon, 1975), elves are ever together, dancing round the faery circle, weaving magics that will shape a better future for all of us. (see our book *Liber Ælph*, 2013b). This is the reason, in part, that we have an eternal kindreth with the Wicca (Silver Elves, 2014) who so often work in groups.

Synchronicity

Elvish magic is not based upon direct cause and effect, that is, asserting one's will upon the universe, as the traditional magician attempts to do when he presents himself as the God of his magic circle. Rather Elvish magic is based upon the harmonious relationship between the elf and the world of spirits and nature. What some might call chance or luck is, as stated previously, the same as saying magic to these elves. Synchronicity is thus the result of the harmonious relationship that elven magic seeks to develop and foster. By synchronicity we mean a-causal events, in the form of coincidences that have created a sense of meaningful impact for the individual. (Jung, 1960a; Aziz, 1990). We elves do not assert our will upon the Universe; rather we seek to induce the spirits, via positive relationship, to fulfill our desires. Just as, say, one might trust that Grandma is disposed to give one something nice for one's birthday. So, too, do we elven trust that the spirits, whom we know to be our kin, will also do their upmost to aid and abet us.

As one begins to come into harmony within one's own being, that is as one begins to merge the conscious and unconscious realms in a harmonious fashion, the chances of synchronistic occurrences increase. One is not only more aware, thus able to more readily perceive meaningful connections; but, being in tune with ones'elf, one becomes inevitably more in harmony with greater nature that then responds to one's wishes and desires. It does this by creating synchronicities. This process might be viewed in a certain sense in the same way that one, upon hearing music, begins to tap one's foot on the floor. We might say that the music causes one to tap one's foot. However, from the elven point of view, the music is not a cause but merely a phenomena to which one is naturally harmonized. So too, when we are in harmony within ours'elves, Nature, and the spirits who abide there, are inclined to tap their feet to our music, the music that is the voice of our soul when it is in harmony, the music of our enchantments.

Creating Synchronicity

It would seem that the title of this section is a paradox. How can one create synchronicity when synchronicity is an a-causal event, and to create, by its nature, indicates an action that is causal. However, we elven create synchronicity by making ours'elves open to it. By harmonizing the elements of our being, by bringing ours'elves into balance, we are optimizing the atmosphere in which synchronicities become possible. We make ours'elves ready, and a harmonious and interconnected Universe replies.

By developing ours'elves as spirits and souls, as human beings, we increase the probability that the harmonious Universe will respond to us and aid us in the attainment of our desires. Efforts to compel our will upon the Universe, while producing some effects, are both limited and exhausting. However, when we put in the effort to develop our own characters people submit of their own will (Wilhelm, 1967) and we obtain what we desire naturally, without strain or effort.

The elves say:

If you do not have the courage to be yourself,

what will you be?

The Wish

One of the keys to elvish magic is the Wish. Traditionally, the elf/faerie folk rewarded those who helped them by granting them a wish. A wish is similar to Will or Intent but is different in that it is an announced desire rather than a concerted effort to compel one's will on a situation. When a wish is combined with action, in this case, the action of s'elf development, the wish becomes magic. That is to say the wish becomes luminous and radiant and thus, like good music, enchants the spirits into tapping their feet along with it, perhaps even getting up to dance. In this way, through time, we obtain by synchronicity and coincidence all that we desire. In many esoteric traditions desire is frowned upon. In Puritan Western cultures desire is most often viewed as being evil and in Buddhism it is seen as an attachment which binds us to life and thus to suffering on the material plane. However, in the *Way of the Wizard*, Deepak Chopra (1995) writes:

Wizards never condemn desire. It was by following their desires that they became wizards. Every desire is created by some past desire. The chain of desire never ends. It is life itself. Don't consider any desire useless or wrong - someday each one will be fulfilled. Desires are seeds waiting for their season to sprout. From a single seed of desire, whole forests grow. Cherish every wish in your heart, however trivial it may seem. One day these trivial wishes will lead you to God. (p. 129)

We elves do more than follow our desires, we wish them into being. For it is our magic to make fantasy reality, to make dreams come true and visions become reality. In other words, we elves use our magic to manifest our vision of a more perfect world.

The Enchantment of the Personal Myth

Welcome to my world. According to Jung (Stein, 1989) the Archetypes and the Collective Unconscious are inherited through our genetic lineage, thus our ancestry. For most of our lives and surely for all the lives of most people, we simply fulfill the aspects of these Archetypes, or myth forming energies, without even realizing what we are doing. However, as we begin to succeed in the process of individuation, we also begin to grasp the notion that the archetypes are permeable and flexible, that is we adjust and change them to fit our own lives. In time we realize that we have the power to transform and create these archetypes. Tolkien (1977a) wrote, "An essential power of Faerie is thus the power of making immediately effective by the will the visions of 'fantasy'". In other words, our power, our art, is to create our own worlds and we do this by becoming our true s'elves and gaining the ability to create and transmutate the archetypal images that have always seemed to rule and guide our lives. They then become, with a mere sprinkling of faerie dust, our servants. In that world, all things enchanting become possible and synchronicity is just another word for elvish magic.

Magical Spells

It is no accident in the elfin mind that the word Spell is used both to mean spelling words and casting magic spells (Soukhanov, 1984). Tolkien (1977a), who was a noted scholar of language as well as an author of fiction, writes, "Small wonder that spell means both a story told, and a formula of power over living men" (p. 35). Words, particularly names, in magical tradition have great power. This thesis is a spell. The pages that you now hold have been instilled with starlight and

101

Elfin magic. It may seep though the pages and enter as invisible light in your eyes and imagination. It may be absorbed by your fingertips and make its way like whispered words of love to your heart and your soul. It is only fair to tell you that if you read any further irrevocable change and transformation will begin, and you will inevitably become who you are truly meant to be.

And now, we go to a greater explanation of the Methods that were used to enter and explore this mythic realm, the realm of the unconscious, the realm of the personal myth.

Some people say

we elves are creatures of myth

and we agree.

We elves are indeed mythic beings,

which ordinary mortals

do well to remember.

CHAPTER 5:
METHODS

"A REAL DREAM MAY INDEED SOMETIMES BE A FAIRY-STORY OF ALMOST ELVISH EASE AND SKILL — WHILE IT IS BEING DREAMED. BUT IF A WAKING WRITER TELLS YOU THAT HIS TALE IS ONLY A THING IMAGINED IN HIS SLEEP, HE CHEATS DELIBERATELY THE PRIMAL DESIRE AT THE HEART OF FAERIE; THE REALIZATION, INDEPENDENT OF THE CONCEIVING MIND, OF IMAGINED WONDER."

(TOLKIEN, 1977A, P. 20)

This has been a study of my Unconscious using the development of my personal myth as a tool of exploration and communication with the unconscious elements of my psyche. I used Depth Methods, which are designed to invite the unconscious to communicate, including Active Imagination (Jung, 1989, Johnson, 1986), Personal Myth (Bond, 1993), Dreamwork (Mindell, 2001, Bosnak, 1988), I Ching (Wilhelm, 1967, Karcher, 1997), Tarot (Hamaker-Zondag, 1997), the Celtic Oracles (Anderson, 1998) and symbolic communications I call Mythic Acts, and Living Dreams, which interpret everyday reality as through it were a dream (Mindell, 2001).

Some people think we elves are fallen angels
but we know we descended into this world on purpose.

Definition of Method

Depth Methods include specific techniques to access, explore and understand hidden or unknown self-experience (McCabe, unpublished manuscript). These methods are designed so as to allow the unconscious to operate and communicate in its own fashion, or language, which is essentially symbolic (Bond, 1993). By allowing the unconscious elements of the Self to communicate in its own way, we gain greater understanding of its point of view and a fuller appreciation for the individual as an entirety. The Depth Methods I chose were selected for one of three specific reasons. Active imagination, personal myth and mythic act were chosen as a means of entering and exploring the unconscious realm from within. The mythic acts were used as a symbolic invitation (Johnson, 1986) to the unconscious to engage in communication and to express itself using the imaginal aspect of active imagination, which is shaped by the environment or setting of my personal myth. The I Ching, Tarot, and Dreams were selected as guides and as tools for communication with the unconscious from consensual reality. That is to say that these oracles were utilized as impartial responses to verify my success and guide my thinking as I endeavored to make sense of the responses I received, often symbolic in nature, of the unconscious. And Living Dreams were utilized as a method of examining events from everyday reality that seemed to be synchronistically in response to the movement of the Personal Myth.

Active Imagination

Active Imagination was developed by Jung (1989) and used by him as a means of interacting with the unconscious. It is a method in which one actively invites the unconscious to dialogue with the conscious mind using imaginal characters that are left free to express themselves. In other words the imagination is given free rein to say whatever it will and whatever comes to one's mind. The guidelines I used for doing Active Imagination are those outlined in Johnson's work (1986). These include inviting the unconscious to communicate, entering the imaginal realm in an established setting (to facilitate the process, in this case the setting of my personal myth), and allowing the imagination to act freely while still preserving the integrity of the ego. By this I mean that the ego does not have to submit to destructive or aggressive elements that may arise from the unconscious and has a right, we may even say a duty, to defend and protect itself. Active imagination is not to be confused with fantasy, which operates freely, easily, and in service of the ego (Raff, 2000). Active imagination is a guided exploration of the unconscious that allows the unconscious to dialogue with the conscious mind (Johnson, 1986).

Active imagination was used in this study as a means of entering into the realm of the unconscious via the imaginal world of my personal myth. It was, in a sense, a primary vehicle for entering my inner world of imagination and meaning.

Personal Myth

Personal Myth (Bond, 1993) was both the vehicle and the setting for my entry into the unconscious. In Carlos Castaneda's (2000) sorcery books the character Don Juan says that to enter the sorcerer's world requires an "incredible feat of perception". Since this was a study of the unconscious via the personal myth, my myth served as both the vehicle and setting for this exploration. All imaginal work took place within the realm of my personal myth, which, as defined by Johnson (1986), is one of the principles upon which successful active imagination depends. My personal myth, which is to say my own understanding of mys'elf as a mythic character, served as a symbolic language that allowed the conscious and unconscious aspects of the psyché to communicate. The details of my personal myth were outlined in the section of the introduction dedicated to the cultural background of my myth.

Living Dreams

Arnold Mindell (2001) in his book the *Dreammaker's Apprentice* suggests that Dreaming occurs at all times and that by observing Consensual Reality in certain ways or by entering Altered States of Consciousness we are able to find "Dreamdoors" (p. 169) into the unconscious. As an extension of this idea, I used what I refer to as Living Dreams in the course of this study. Living Dreams, by that I mean I examined what occurred while I was in the Mythic Act (see below) and its aftereffects, as though they were a dream. While these events took place outwardly in what is Consensual Reality, the interpretation of them was done from the perspective of the Personal Myth. That is to say the mythic acts were a real events, taking place in the outer world, and observable to anyone passing by. However, the meaning of these acts and the interpretation of any effects of the acts were analyzed in accordance with my Personal Myth and not from the point of view of consensual or normal reality or, if we were to speak in terms of the Harry Potter books, from the Muggles' point of view. It is a view from the inside of the myth and magic rather than the outside.

The mode of interpretation I used was in the associative style of Bosnak (1988) and Johnson (1986) wherein elements of the mythic acts were treated as symbols, just as in a dream. Then, those symbols were examined for personal and mythic associations in order to draw meaning from them. By personal association, I mean those aspects of a dream that call to mind experiences from my own life. By mythic associations, I mean connections that stem from traditionally held beliefs about symbolic meaning, such as the ocean being frequently interpreted to represent the unconscious.

I also used and depended on what Jeremy Taylor (1983) calls "the tingle" as to what interpretation seemed right to me. The tingle is an intuitive or instinctive response that a particular interpretation is meaningful or correct. It touches something within the dreamer, and it was the primary mode I used for choosing between possible interpretations.

The dreams used were chosen because they were either incubated, that is, I specifically asked for a dream in response to a question and accepted whatever dream I had as the answer, or a dream that occurred spontaneously after the Mythic Acts (see below) and had elements that clearly designated it as a response to the invocation of the Mythic Acts.

I Ching

When someone once commented that the ancient Chinese had no scientific method, Jung (1962) replied that they did in fact have a scientific method and that it was to be found in the I Ching. Since entering into the unconscious has its dangers (Jung, 1956) and since there was a possibility of error in my interpretation of its communications, I used the I Ching (Wilhelm, 1967, Karcher, 1997) as an independent tool for confirming or challenging my insights about my experience there. The I Ching, then, could be regarded as the scientific method of the unconscious. The I Ching is composed of 64 hexagrams, each containing six lines, anyone one of which, or any combination of lines, can change to its opposite. Therefore, any one of the 64 hexagrams can change to any of the others, thus creating a sense of transformation or process. The I Ching utilizes a random selection process. (Von Franz, 1980). The hexagram is drawn by splitting a pile of 48 sticks (in the elven tradition in which I was trained, others use 50.) into two sections and counting out one of the two. It is its randomness that allows the unconscious to enter in and express itself. Thus it was used as a means of double-checking the conclusions of the conscious mind about its interactions with the unconscious psyché. The I Ching acts on the principle of synchronicity (Jung, 1960a), which is defined as a non-causal or a-causal meaningful coincidence. The idea is that a random throw of the I Ching gives us relevant information concerning the event we are asking about at the time we are inquiring. It was also used in the study as a method of timing, that is, I did the I Ching to get an idea about the auspiciousness of beginning a particular activity or, if it so indicated, to delay an activity. In other words, the question to the I Ching was very often, is this the right time?

Tarot

The Tarot is similar to the I Ching, in that it is also used as an oracle, but unlike the I Ching, has little in the way of definite textual meaning. It relies more on the interpreter's impression of symbolic images. It was used therefore as a guide and a tool of communication with the unconscious, giving hints about how I might have viewed or perceived certain events, as well as, giving suggestions at certain points in how I was to proceed. It is a symbolic language displayed on cards, combining both pictures and generally accepted and personally developed associative meanings. However, the tarot acts in many ways like dreams, which speak symbolically but leave the interpretation to the conscious mind.

108

Again, like the I Ching, the value of the Tarot rests on the theory of synchronicity. There is an assumption that whatever answer one receives is the right or relevant response. It is important to understand that the Tarot, the I Ching, the Celtic Oracles and other oracular devices used, while they are based on Jung's theory of synchronicity (Hopcke, 1997), are not being offered here as a method of Jungian psychology but rather as a method of my personal myth. There is no claim here of the scientific validity of these methods, but within the realm of my personal myth they are seen as being completely valid.

From the point of view of psychology, these tools were used as a means of prompting a response from the unconscious, which then would offer images and thoughts to guide their interpretation. However, from the point of view of my personal myth, these tools are seen as devices of communication with the realm of the spirits, which are projected as being outside, rather than, interior to my consciousness. This is in keeping with a shamanic view of the world (Larsen, 1988), which is to say an animistic worldview, in which, all things are alive with consciousness.

Also, along with the Tarot, I used several other Tarot like card decks including the Secret Dakini Oracle (Douglas, Slinger, 1979), the Druid Animal Oracle (Carr-Gomm, 1994) and the Celtic Shaman's Pack (Matthews, 1995).

Celtic Oracles

The Celtic Oracles (Anderson, 1998) became an integral part of my study. I had not intended them to be so, but they were pointed out to me, via numinous experience, and proved invaluable in my process of exploring the inner world of my psyché. Like the I Ching, they consist of 64 possible basic results, but which are arrived at by a process of throwing two coins, three times. (Unlike the I Ching, where we used sticks, although one can use coins and if so one throws three coins six times.)

What made this particular oracle so valuable was its basic Celtic/Faery mythology. Its interpretations were perfectly in keeping with the cultural assumptions of my personal myth and helped guide me in both gauging the success of a particular activity, such as the mythic acts or active imagination, and in suggesting new activities or directions for me to explore.

The Mythic Acts

I had a quandary on what to call this method. I could have called it *Ritual*, but Ritual implies a repeated act and thus did not entirely fit, While my acts were numerous, they were not entirely repetitions of each other. I could have called it *Ceremonies* but the acts were not always ceremonial. I could have called it *Shamanic Exploration*, however, the elements that are so often a part of shamanic journeying, that is to say dance, drumming and/or trance inducing herbs were not, in every instance, utilized in this study. Nor did I explore the vertical world, a world of under and over worlds, that is the shamanic landscape (Larsen, 1996). (Note how this shamanic landscape is similar to the ancient Norse worldview of the Yggdrasil tree. (Larrington, 1999).) I considered using the term *Altered States of Consciousness*, but again the dreamwork examined not only the altered state but also the resonance from the field (Feinstein, 1998) that followed. I decided instead to call it *Mythic Acts*. Mythic Acts are symbolic acts, much in a form of a mini theatrical play, in which a communication of intent is relayed to the psyché and the unconscious using its own language, which is symbolic, mythic and imaginal (Larsen, 1996).

It should be noted that from the point of view of the Personal Myth and my unconscious, that this section is more accurately called the Magical Acts or the Enchantments. I make this distinction because magic is generally conceived of as a process of using the laws of Nature and the Universe to compel events to occur, but enchantment as a magic, by our definition, is rather a process of enticing or intriguing someone in order to achieve a particular outcome. Thus it is most proper to note that in this study I enchanted the unconscious to communicate and made no effort to compel it to do so. The unconscious was thus treated with the same respect that one would treat any person with whom one wished to communicate. Larsen (1996) tells us, "The unconscious seems to be involved with our concerns, but it is no mere physical mirror, rather ... it is a magical one." (p. 116). In other words, the unconscious has its own worldview, which is magical in nature, and it is that view that I endeavored to elicit in this study by use of its own language, the language of myth, symbol and magic.

In performing the mythic/magical/enchanted act, I was in effect living in two worlds at the same time. I performed the act in the world of consensual reality, that is to say anyone observing could see exactly what I was doing. However, the acts themselves were of the mythic realm and were symbolic communications to that realm. It was in this way that I was living my myth. The mythic acts, or enchantments or magical acts, were actually done, not simply imagined. They became real in that way. Thus they became a communication to the psyché or spirit world, not simply as something imagined, but as something embodied.

It may be noted by some that in engaging in the mythic or magical act I was, in fact, entering into the developmental phase that Piaget (1950) said was denoted by superstitious or magical thinking. And this is exactly the case. To enter the mythic realm, I had to enter it on its own terms, and those terms are magical. Avens (1982) said, "The world of the primitive is fully alive because it is neither purely subjective nor purely objective, neither spiritual nor material, but ensouled." (p. 69). Thus I had to ensoul the myth in order to treat it with the respect and validity that it deserves.

Biases

This study takes the basic view of shamanism that the imaginal world is every bit as real in its own way as the world of consensual reality (Harner, 1982, Mindell, 2001). However, it also makes a distinction between the imaginal and fantasy, as so designated in the works of Johnson (1986) and Raff (2000). The fantasy realm is devoted to the wish fulfillment needs of the ego and the persona. The imaginal realm, however, is the voice of the unconscious psyché and does not necessarily agree with nor fulfill the wishes of the conscious self. It is an independent aspect of the individual with its own needs and point of view.

I also make an assumption that the Personal Myth is most valid and thus empowering when composed of experiences from consensual reality rather than exclusively the fantasy realm. Since the fantasy realm seeks to fulfill a real need or desire with an imagined response or activity, it does not have the power or sense of validity that an actual event does. For instance, I could imagine eating an apple, which would give some satisfaction to my mind or body but not as much as if, after imagining eating an apple, I actually ate one. Real events give validity to the personal myth that cannot be had from fantasy alone. However, it was not the purpose of this paper to present evidence that this is so but merely an a priori assumption used when composing the elements of my personal myth.

I also make a basic assumption that the oracles received, using I Ching, Celtic Oracles, etc., were an accurate communication from the spirit world or the unconscious. It is not the purpose of this study to test or question the validity of these oracles. Any errors are to be viewed as a failure on my part as interpreter, not as a failure of the oracle itself.

In our next chapter we will detail the use of these methods and the results and responses that occurred in these encounters with the unconscious and my exploration of the inner world of myth and meaning.

Elves do not seek

to make waves in the world.

The fact that some folks are surprised,

even shocked, to see us

says more about them than us.

Yet to our minds,

the fact that they see us at all

is a good sign that humanity is

Awakening.

The Oceans remind the elves
of our home in Faerie.
The Forests remind us
of our home as well,
as do the Mountains.
The cities of Man, however,
remind us that humanity is
at least a bit insane
and to be therefore cautious around them.

CHAPTER 6:

ENTERING ELFIN:

AN INTEGRATED IMAGINAL PROCESS

> *"THERE IS NO FAERIE BUT FAERIE, AND IT IS NOT THERE BUT HERE."*
> *(WAITE, 1974, P. 164)*

Reminder

In this chapter I depart from the psychological perspective for the most part and enter and write from the point of view of my personal myth. While most of what I am about to say has been covered more fully in the previous chapter on Methods, I think it might be helpful at this point if I remind the reader of a few things to keep in mind while reading this chapter.

First, this is a Depth Method Inquiry. Depth Methods are used to enter into communication with and invite a response from the unconscious aspects of the psyché. This chapter then is a communication with and from my psyché. However, it should be remembered that within my Personal Myth the psyché is not exclusive to a subjective response of my unconscious but includes the assumption of a spirit world as a real, living and viable entity and in particular that the world called Faerie is a real/spiritual realm. By spirit world we mean a psyché and psychés that exist beyond my own being and inhabit the natural world as living, although mostly invisible, entities. In this way we may conceive that my inner world, my unconscious is the doorway to the vast unknown that exists beyond my conscious awareness.

Second, several oracles are used as a representation of the communication of those spirits. They are assumed to be an accurate communication from that world. Oracles, let me remind the reader, are randomly drawn responses to a specific or general question dependent on the process of synchronicity. While I make no claim to their scientific validity, within the process of my personal myth, that is, within this chapter, they are assumed to be accurate and sincere communications from the world of the spirits. To understand this fully one needs to suspend one's disbelief.

Third, there is a slightly erotic tone to my active imaginal process that might make some readers uncomfortable, and the members of my thesis committee asked me to speak to the issue of whether the erotic has a place in an academic study. To answer this question, I think we must ask ourselves whether in studying the unconscious we need to censor its contents. If say, I had a dream in which I appeared naked in front of a group of people, would I then clothe myself in my report of the dream? Or if I had sex in a dream, would I then not mention that detail when interpreting it? The fact is that the contents of my unconscious, as it appeared during this process, turned out to be slightly erotic, and the dialogue contained within the active imaginational process is accented by sexual innuendo. This is a fact of my psyche. To my mind, to alter, censor or dress up the response of my psyche is to abnegate my responsibility as a psychological scientist. If we are to study the psyche as scientists then, in my opinion at least, we must study it for what it is, not what we wish it to be.

What follows is a full and accurate reportage of my depth process and the response of my psyche as I entered into and lived my personal myth over a month's time. It is a complete and unaltered record. Nothing has been added nor detracted, except some details that were revealed in previous explorations of that realm (prior to this study) that will give increased understanding of the individuals and the locations described. I have laid my psyché bare before you, and I can only ask that you, the reader, consider it with an open mind.

Finally, it might be noted that while my Personal Myth does not exclude the validity of the psychological perspective, it is not limited by it. This is in keeping with my thesis that the personal myth is most effective when lived as an integrated aspect in consensual reality. That is to say one is aware of the commonly held views of society while not necessarily conforming to them. From here on out in this chapter I move into the realm of the personal myth, which in my case is a realm traditionally called Faerie. I hope you enjoy the journey.

Timing

It has been so difficult to start this part of my thesis. I've had an incredible resistance to beginning the Active Imagination or the Acts of Magic, which is curious because this is the part I've been looking forward to doing. However, I've felt I've had no energy for doing so. Curiously though, I've been working vigorously on the rest of this thesis, the more mundane parts, that are so much less inviting to me.

I've asked myself, is the time not right? Like nearly all things, magic is, in part, a matter of timing. However, also like nearly everything else in life, circumstances often prevent one from waiting for the perfect time, and one must make do with the best time to act, all things considered.

Or perhaps, I am simply low on energy. Is this lack of energy due to some inner resistance or is it actually my body's way of saying the time has not yet come? After weeks of low energy, I decided to ask the I Ching (Wilhelm, 1967) if the time had at

117

last come to begin this part of the study. I received hexagram number one, the Creative that says, "When an individual draws this oracle, it means that success will come to him from the primal depths of the universe and that everything depends upon his seeking his happiness and that of others in one way only, that is, by perseverance in what is right" (p. 4). This is an oracle of power and spirit and I take it to mean that the way is opening for me to proceed, with the caveat that whatever I do should be guided by my own moral and spiritual understanding.

Eldafaryn

However, although I did the oracle I still couldn't find the energy to proceed. Consciously I wish to proceed but my unconscious, as evidenced by my feeling sense is still reluctant. It was the next evening when I finally decided to walk among the trees that live in Eldafaryn and speak to them of this issue. Eldafaryn, which means Elf Haven, is the name of our home and of an astral realm that surrounds it that moves with us whenever we relocate. At the time of this study, it was bounded by a park to the south, a creek to the east, and open field where lies the Realm of Nathandyryn (see figure 1, page 219) to the north and, to the west, a hillside rising toward a small mountain.

As I walked the length of my realm, I greeted the trees, sent energy into the areas of magic until finally, energized by their being I had enough energy to return home and proceed with a journey into Elfin. However, before I reveal my journey, let me tell you a story that bears upon these matters, for it tells of one of the guides I shall use in proceeding and how I came to choose it.

A Curious Sign

A funny thing happened on my way to my thesis approval meeting with my committee. As I was about to enter the room where the meeting was to take place, Professor Victor Daniels (2003), co- author (with his wife, Kooch) of *Tarot D'Amour* stopped me and asked if I was the tarot reader. (Silver Flame, Lyndaryel and I had taught a 101 Psychology class that used Tarot, I Ching and magical theory as a means of teaching Jung's theories.) I said I was, and he then escorted me to his office where he gifted me with a signed copy of their book. I took this as a sign, but what did it mean? A sign, yes, but a sign of what? I considered the idea that it was a sign that I should consider his and his wife's book as a tool in my thesis. However, upon examination, while I like their book very much and think it is intriguing and well written, I couldn't see how it would quite fit into my thesis.

Previously, I had asked Professor Susan Stewart if I could borrow a book from her entitled *Celtic Oracles* (Anderson, 1998), which I had seen at her home but had never had a chance to do more than scan briefly. She brought the book with her to my thesis committee meeting that day, and after examining it I came to the conclusion that the sign had actually been to point out that oracle, not *Tarot D'Amour*. I know this interpretation must seem curious, but then I am an elf, and our reasoning is often paradoxical to others.

Choosing the Celtic Oracles

Therefore I decided to use the Celtic Oracles (Anderson, 1998) as a guide in my process. After receiving the Creative in the I Ching, I cast the Celtic Oracle and received number 36 the Cauldron of the Otherworld (Anderson, 1998), which speaks of

"Invoking Healing and Replenishing the Spirit" (p. 131). This seemed to me to be a very valid and accurate response to the almost total lack of energy I had been feeling. I took this to indicate that my first duty was to enter Elfin, through the realm of Nathandyryn, the world where I commonly go in Active Imagination, in order to drink from the chalice of healing and revive my energy.

Note that in proceeding that this was not my first effort at Active Imagination and I had previously entered the realm of Nathandyryn and knew some of the residents thereof. However, those explorations are not included in this book and were not a part of this study.

Procedure

My procedure for entering Active Imagination involved sitting alone in a quiet room in our house, entering a meditative, semi-trance state, and imagining my astral body (Powell, 1927), body of light, or etheric double as it is often called in esoteric circles. I would imagine this body as a double of my physical body, with the addition of pointed ears and a bit more hair on top than I currently have, and experience it rising from the physical, looking back at my prone or seated body and then turning around and leaving the room.

This first part, looking at my physical body proved to be the most difficult thing each time and I endeavored to do it as effortlessly as possible, attempting to incorporate the ease of fantasizing with the activity and effort of imaginal work. This is also, in part, why these explorations have a slightly flirting, romantic, sexual tone to them. Most of my life I have fantasized about sex and romantic encounters, they come easy to me. I also fantasize about stories I might write, adventures in short stories or novels. Most I never write but I cannot seem to help but fantasize about them, imagining the characters, their actions, conversations, etc. By incorporating these elements in my active imagination, I seek to make it easier, for I know if I don't do so, I will soon give up doing it.

From there I would walk in this astral body to our living room whose walls were lined on two sides with wide bookshelves that spanned nearly the entire wall, and on which we had not only books and over 50 tarot decks but some of the 500+ figurines of elves, faeries, pixies, gnomes and many other beings that housed our teraphim (household spirits). In my imagination, the bookshelf farthest from the bedroom where my physical body sat opened as a portal to Nathandyryn, the elvish realm whose physical presence lay just across the main road from which one would turn to get to our house. Only, in the imaginal realm, there was no road, nor a sidewalk bordering it, merely wild nature that held the dwellings of an elven community. However, the field, the stream and the great oak tree and most of the natural elements of the place, still existed in its imaginal counterpart.

Once I came to the portal in our living room, I would step through it and be transported immediately to the edge of Nathandyryn, which in physical world terms would have taken about a five-minute walk. I could have taken this walk in my imagination, but choose not to do so. Somehow, stepping through this portal helped me understand I was stepping into another realm of being. Once there, the portal would dissolve behind me until that time that I would return to it and step back into my living room, walk to my physical body and reenter it. The portal would reappear when I intended to use it. I used this same method for entering Nathandyryn every time I went there; save in a few cases when I was away from home and would imagine a portal in some magic spot wherever I happened to be.

The Chalice of Healing, 1 - 03 - 2005, Active Imagination

I enter Nathandyryn at the gate near Alyryn's house. Alyryn and his twin sister Anathea, live in a house tucked into the trees and covered in vines near the creek that runs along the eastside of Nathandyryn (Anathea also has a tree house on the other side of the creek. Unlike most people in the normal world, elves continually share their homes with friends frequently coming, going and staying.). I don't know why I decided to go there exactly. I was thinking of going to see Enderea, who lives in a tree house farther north along the edge of the forest and still to the west of the creek, but at the last moment I came here instead. It is dark out, and there is a light on in Alyryn's house, and from its far side a flickering, as from a fire.

I open his door, the doors here are always unlocked; in fact, I don't think they have locks, and I peek in but not seeing anyone, call out "hello." I receive no answer but can see through the glass of the back door that there are elves gathered in the back yard. I pass through and find there are about a dozen or so, sitting and standing around a campfire.

"What's this?" someone calls out, and then I see Alyryn, his long blond white hair reflecting the firelight, as he comes toward me. He grasps me by both my arms, just beneath the elbows, and I his in kind. He says, "Welcome, brother," and then turning to the others says, "Look who's come, the Lord of Eldafaryn."

There are congenial greetings like a chorus from around the fire, which I return with a wave and hellos. One among them rises, and I see that it is Anathea, Alyryn's twin sister, with long white hair to match his own. She comes from the far side of the fire circle and advances to me, pausing just beyond arms' reach.

"It's been a while," she says.

"Yes," I agreed, "It always seems that way, doesn't it?"

122

"I'm glad you've come," she says and then a smile spreads across her beautiful face, and she steps closer and taking hold of my coat pulls me to her. She stokes my face with her right hand, and then reaching up on tiptoes, for she is a bit shorter than I, she kisses me upon the lips, a lingering kiss that I admit I have sorely missed.

"So," she says, stepping back and taking me by the hand, "Come tell me all. Is this a social call or is there purpose in your coming?"

"Purpose yes, " say I, following her around the fire. "And social as well, always social, for I have longed to see you, yet have not felt the strength to come."

"That other world drains you, that's for sure," she comments. "But tell me what purpose is so strong that you do come now when you had not the strength before?"

"That is the strange part," I reply, as we settle on the far side of the fire. "I came to get the strength to come."

She eyes me curiously and laughs and comments, "Wizards!"

"I've come to drink from the cauldron of renewal. I've come to drink from the chalice of healing."

"Have you, indeed?" says she. And then she nods her head as though she's thought something over and come to a decision, and she asks, "Now? You would do this now?"

"Whenever I can," I reply.

And she nods again then calls out, "Alyryn," who glances up at her. "See you later," she says and he nods and smiles. "Good night, all of you," she calls to the others and then to me, "Well, let's go, shall we?" And she takes me by the hand and leads me north through the forest.

"How's Adana?" I ask as we proceed. Adana is another elf I've come to know here, who lives in a treehouse on the other side of the creek. Anathea has a house in the same tree.

"Missing you," she replies, "like all of us. But her particularly. She has a thing for you, you know."

"I have a thing for her as well," I say.

And she replies, "Yes, and she's sorely missed it," and smirks. "And so have I," she adds, and then she sighs and says, "Alas, we must make do with beautiful young lads."

"I'm sure that's hard on you," I say.

"Harder than you realize," she says, then adds, "No pun intended."

"Where are we going?" I inquire.

"The pool," says she, "The spring of healing. I thought you were there once before?"

"I was," I admitted. "I was just wondering if that's where you were taking me."

"If it wasn't so cold I'd take you right here," she says.

"Would you?"

"In a heartbeat," she responds.

"I would it would last longer."

"As long as you wish," says she. Then stopping and pulling me close to her, she kisses me again, and we linger in each other's arms while our heated breath makes clouds of mist about us.

"Come." She takes my hand again, and we proceed onward.

We come to Enderea's, and I say, "I wonder if she's here."

"Let's find out," says Anathea and pulls on a vine that hangs from the branches where Enderea's tree house resides. I hear a bell ring from above. A moment later, Enderea's voice calls down from the balcony, "Who is it?"

"It is I, sweet princess," says Anathea, stepping into the light cast from Enderea's open door. "And look, I've brought your prince," she says as she pulls me into the light as well.

Enderea's long red hair hangs about her face as she peers over her balcony and says, "I take it you're not coming up."

Anathea shakes her head and tells her, "We're headed to the pool. Our prince needs replenishing, it seems."

"I'll be right down, " says Enderea and then retreats into her house and emerges a moment later wearing a dark velvet cloak, perhaps blue or black or even dark green, although in the shadows of the night and the forest I can't really tell. Then I can hear her feet on the steps that wind in the hollow of the tree she lives on, clipping quickly downward. A moment later, she emerges and approaches us.

"Sister," she says, as she kisses Anathea, and then turning to me she says, "And you, at last," and she kisses me on my forehead, my eyes and my lips. "So to the pool," she says. "So be it." Then she cups her hands around her mouth and screeches like an owl several times. Shortly thereafter an owl flutters down to a nearby branch, and she speaks to it in a series of screeches and clicks until a moment later, it flies off.

"Ready," she declares and takes my right hand as Anathea takes my left, and we proceed north again through the trees.

"So how are things in Eldafaryn?" She asks as we walk.

"Well," I reply, "Very well."

"But our scouts say you have not been out at night much. Not since Elfie passed over." Elfie was our elven wolfhound who had recently died.

"It's true," I admitted. "He was a great excuse for late night walks. How is he?" I ask, for when Elfie passed, he passed into Nathandyryn. (His spirit now lives with us in Hawaii.)

"Well," she says, " and happy. Perhaps you'll see him sometime. I know he'd be glad to see you."

All this time, we've been walking near the bank of the creek, but here it turns to the east while we continue to the north, the earth rising slightly before us. Steam and mist are thick here, and climbing up the slight rise before us, I realize why. The pool's hot breath is steaming the air.

"So here we are," announces Enderea. Then looking at me she says, "Come, I'll help you take your clothes off."

"Are you kidding?" I ask. "It's cold out here."

"But the pool is warm, my love, and you must bathe in the waters of purification before you drink of the sacred waters of life, healing and rejuvenation. Come," she says, "Here, we'll join you." And she and Anathea begin to shed their clothes and I feel I have no choice but to do the same.

Once naked, we descend into the misting waters of the pool until we are covered up to our chests (and for Anathea, her shoulders). Enderea scoops water in her hands and pours it over my head, saying, "I anoint you with the sacred waters. I wash away the unbidden past that would cling to you." Then she takes the water and wipes it over my face and neck, as though washing me tenderly.

I begin to notice light flickering on the other side of the hill that we have just crossed and soon realize these are candles held by seven elf maids, dressed in dark purple velvet robes, who now surround the pool. By their light, I can now see that there is a statue of an elven lady on the far side of the water, to the north, opposite from where we have come. She is naked and unadorned except for a chalice that she holds in her hands and a jewel that reflects the candlelight on her forehead. To her left, our right as we face her, is a low rock cliff from which water trickles in a small stream into the pool. (I realize alerting these attendants of the sacred pool was the mission upon which Enderea sent the owl.)

Enderea wades to that side of the pool, climbs upon the rocks there, takes the chalice from the hands of the statue and fills it from the trickling stream. Then, when it is full, she waves to me and I wade over and climb the rock to stand beside her and despite the fact that I am now standing naked in the chill night air, I am not cold in the least, the heat of the pool having penetrated deep into my bones.

She lifts the chalice and waves her hand over it, saying something in a voice so low, I cannot hear. Then she offers it to me, saying, "This is the sacred chalice of life. Drink of life. Drink of immortality."

As I take the chalice, she caresses my left cheek and then leans toward me, kisses me gently on the lips and says again, "Drink of life. Drink of immortality," and the others standing around the pool and Anathea within it, intone the words after her.

I lift the cup up to my forehead, offering it to the spirits and then to my lips, drinking fully from it.

"Drink it all," she instructs me and I do so, its heat like hot tea warming my insides. Anathea has now climbed upon the rock behind me and embraces me, her cheek pressed against my back.

"You are sacred to me," said Enderea and taking the chalice from my hand, presses hers'elf against me and kisses me deeply. Then pulling back she smiles and says, "Done, my sweet lord," and she returns the chalice to the statue's hand. "Thank you, sisters," she says to the acolytes, who bow to her, blow out their candles and disappear into the forest.

A while later, we wade back through the pool and find robes with hoods that have been left for us, which we don. We gather our clothes and make our way back to Enderea's where we dry off before dressing again.

"And how do you feel now?" Enderea asks me.

"Better, " I say. "I feel like something has shifted."

"It will take a little time," she tells me. "It is not sudden, but it is certain and the more enduring for its gradualness."

"And if it helps you come back to us..." says Anathea.

"Yes," I say, "I should be returning soon."

"You always say that," Enderea points out, but she is not being cross so much as wise and knowing.

"And I always mean it," I reply. "But not always able to do it."

"Well, this time, let it be so," says Anathea and she reaches over and squeezes my hand.

"Yes," I say, "let it be so."

Then they walk me to the gateway (there is more than one portal here) that is in the field near Enderea's, who says, "Good-bye, sweet lover."

"Soon, soon," says Anathea. A wish? An order? A hope?

"As soon as I can," I promise, and step through the gateway and return to the normal world, or as normal as my day-to-day life of an eccentric tends to be.

The Follow Up

The question is now, did the Active Imagination have the desired effect? Will going to the pool and drinking from the chalice revitalize my energy? Time will be one indication, but another way to quickly get an answer is to ask the oracle again and see what it tells me. So I do the Celtic Oracles again, asking if it has an impression of the results of the Active Imagination.

I receive number 59, entitled Oengus/Mabon, Youthful Champion, Son of Light which says, "Whatever your age, the oracle promises you a youthful energy to champion an honorable cause, action, and outcome" (Anderson, 1998, p. 203). Because the text speaks of youthful energy I take it to mean that indeed the revitalization of my energy has begun. And in fact, the next day, I feel greatly revitalized and spend the entire day working on my thesis as well as my other duties and projects.

Sun Wheel

The question then becomes, what do I do next? I again inquire of the Celtic Oracles book and this time I receive number 63, which is called Sun Wheels. It speaks of "Invoking the Quality of Protection" (Anderson 1998, p. 213). It tells of sun wheels that were signs of healing and protection, which were put on talismans and amulets and were often "offered at healing springs and lakes...." (p. 213).

So from this I surmise two things. First, that I should create a Sun Wheel talisman (see figure 2, page 220) and second, that I should carry it in Active Imagination to the pool in Nathandyryn and offer it to the spirits there.

The Talisman

I have some small stones that I collected from Dylyn beach where the elf princess Suzynsu resides. (Suzynsu is the elven name I have given to Professor Susan Stewart. In her own mind, she is perhaps merely a psychologist and a professor thereof. But in my personal myth, my way of seeing and interacting with the world, I experience her as an elven princess.) These stones have been lying in my garage since last summer and are now, in mid-winter, nearly freezing to the touch. I choose one from among them, and I place it outside in the sunlight. It has been raining for nearly two weeks straight, and this is the first day there has been any sun at all. After several hours, however, the stone is warm to the touch.

Having instilled it with sunlight, I now paint the symbol of a radiant sun in gold on one side. I am doing this while the stone is still bathed in light. After that, I paint an outline of the golden glyph in yellow. Now I have my basic talisman of the sun wheel, and the work of instilling it with magic begins. (Nine

129

years later, we still keep it on our magic table. A magic table is what these elves call what most would refer to as an altar. Because of the religious connotations of altar, we choose the term magic table instead; although it you called it *alter*, we'd probably agree with you.)

Tobacco

Spirits require energy and attention. They must be fed to be able to do their work properly, just as we do. Tobacco is one means of feeding them. Narby writes that the Amazon forest shamans believe that tobacco is the grandchild of the spirit world (Narby, 1998). For the last five years, as indicated earlier, I've been growing my own tobacco and rolling its leaves into cigars for shamanic work. Now, I take one of these cigars and blow the smoke upon the sun-wheel stone, invoking the spirits while visualizing the card I draw about the stone from the Secret Dakini Oracle (Douglas, Slinger, 1979), which is Serpent Power that speaks of "An awakening of latent powers" (p. 130). The tobacco serves as a food and attractant for the spirits. Remember, enchantment is greatly about attraction.

The Offering 1 - 06 - 05, Active Imagination

Now it is time to take the stone and offer it at the pool. I enter Nathandyryn at the gateway near Enderea's and begin walking north across the field that is encircled on three sides by the forest. I'm heading again to the sacred pool of healing. I see some elves off to my left on the far side of the field but do not recognize them and continue on.

Someone calls out, "Hey," from off to my right, and I see an elf maid with a smiling face peek out from the woods. She waves to me but then, laughing, retreats. Again, she is not someone I recognize. I reach into my left pants pocket where I'm carrying the sun wheel stone, (its etheric double, really) and grasp it in my hand and then release it again. The field is still wet from rains, and my feet sink a little with each step I take. The north edge of the field, which is the beginning of the forest, looms directly ahead of me.

It is evening, and there is still light enough to see, but it becomes immediately darker as I enter the forest. I pause now and can hear murmured voices, but can't tell from which direction they originate. I continue on toward the pool, and as I do so the land begins to rise, and once again I can see the misty steam rising ahead of me from beyond the embankment where I know the pool resides. As I climb the rise, I can see the faint flicker of lights ahead of me. Now upon the rise I see candles flicker on the rocks about the pool and within it a couple bathing in the heat.

"Good evening," I say and the elfin couple turns to see me now and return my greeting in kind. "I didn't mean to disturb you."

"You're welcome, brother," says the male elf and the female adds, "All are welcome here. Join us, please."

So I shed my clothes quickly, because of the night fast approaching with its growing chill, and I slip the stone into my hand and wade into the pool.

"I won't disturb you long," I say, "I've just brought a gift for the spirit of the pool."

"Oh, yes? " says the elf maid, her shoulder length brown hair hanging wet upon her head. "Can we see?"

"Indeed, " says the male, whose black hair is drawn back into a pony tail, "Would you mind?"

"Not at all," I reply, "But it's quite a simple thing," and I present the stone to them.

"A Sun Wheel," says the elf maid, "Did you make it?" When I tell her I did she says, "It's very nice. It's an ancient tradition, " she adds, "I suppose you know that."

"Well," I admit, "I newly know it."

"The candles are the same in their way," the male elf tells me. "But a temporary offering rather than a permanent one like this," he says, referring to the stone.

"I'm Zardoa, by the way," I say.

"Treandre," says the female introducing hers'elf, and the male says, "Vyndarys."

Treandre asks, "Do you live in Nathandyryn?"

"No," I reply, "Eldafaryn, just south of here."

"I think I've heard of it," she says and then laughs merrily, her candle lit face illuminated by joy.

"Where do you plan to put the stone?" Vyndarys asks.

"I thought at the feet of the statue," I answer.

"Seems good," Vyndarys says, and they both nod.

"Perhaps you would meditate while I place the stone," I suggest. They both replied in the affirmative. I wade to the far side of the pool, climb upon the rock, bow before the statue, blow upon the stone my intention of healing and protection and then kneel on my right knee as I place it at the statue's unshod feet. Then I rise, place my hand upon my heart, bow my head and return to the pool, climbing slowing in so there is almost no splash.

"It feels good," says Treandre when I return to them.

"It does," agrees Vyndarys.

"Thank you," I say and begin to wade to the edge of the pool.

"No need to go," Vyndarys tells me.

"Oh," I say, "I think it best if I leave you to your whisperings." And Treandre laughs, her brown eyes sparkling, as she does so. "Do you have a towel?" She asks me.

"Alas, I do not," I confess.

"Use one of ours," says Vyndarys, "Up there on the bank," he adds and inclines his head in that direction.

"I couldn't."

"Of course, you could," he replies.

"What will you do?"

They look at each other and laugh and she says, "We'll share the other one."

"I really couldn't," I say again.

"You shared the magic with us," says Vyndarys, "Now let us share with you."

I nod to them and emerge from the pool. I climb to the right and find the towels upon the bank and take the top one saying, "Thanks." Just at that moment, as I turn to thank them, I see a white form emerge above the statue on the far bank. Treandre and Vyndarys follow my gaze and turn to see a white stag standing upon the mossy rise.

Treandre gasps and blurts, "Sacred stars."

The stag seems to stare right into me; and then, a moment later, turns and disappears into the forest. I'm amazed, and Vyndarys says, "A great sign for you, my friend, and a blessing for us as well."

After that we are silent. It is as though we have been touched deeply by something profoundly sacred. I dry myself off, put on my clothes, nod good-bye and head back toward the gateway, thinking all the while about, and still amazed, perhaps entranced, by the visitation.

Waiting

When I do the Celtic Oracles again, to verify the results of my efforts, I receive number 4, the Sacred Three, which speaks of "Awareness of the Spirit World" (Anderson, 1998, p. 31). It says, "You are focusing too narrowly on the immediate circumstances rather than looking at the larger context and possibilities for the future" (p. 31-32).

Now I have a dilemma. I have clearly missed something, but don't know what. When I ask the various oracles about this, I keep getting indications that I just need to wait and that the spirit world will speak to me in some fashion but I'm not clear how. Will an event occur? Perhaps a dream? I'm filled with energy now and find it difficult to be patient. However, in the last several days I had been writing and typing so much and with such passion that I have ignored signals from my body that my right arm was growing stressed and now can barely type at all. So the wait has a practical aspect as well; it has come at the right time.

However, I feel driven and still want to do something, even if it is to go forth at night and converse with the trees. But every time I start to go out and do so the pouring rain drives me back in. I'm held in check by the spirit world, and there is naught I can do but compose myself.

The Dream

Three nights later I have a dream. Most of it is hazy, but the best I can remember is that I am part of a group that has just pulled a heist in England. We are in the upstairs of a warehouse, celebrating by having an indoor barbecue. Someone has betrayed us to the police, and I see him on the floor getting a knife put through his throat. Now, however, the police will be
134

coming soon, and his body is the only evidence against us, and we're trying to figure out a way to dispose of it before the police arrive. All this is rather hazy, but the next part of the dream stands out vividly in my mind. As I'm looking about for a solution to the difficulty, I see a huge piece of meat, like an enormous pot roast, cooking on the grill. It reaches out a part of itself, like an arm with no hand, and waves to me. I realize it is telling me to cut up the traitor and roast him on the barbecue, perhaps even offer him in this unrecognizable state (according to the dream) to the police.

Now I could attempt to analyze the entire dream but as I said most of it is vague and, in essence and content, not unlike a hundred movies I have seen. However, the roast waving to me stands out so vividly in my mind that I conclude that it contains the essence, the kernel of the message and it is that portion of the dream I ponder.

What could it possibly mean for a dead piece of meat, roasting on a grill to signal to me? And it comes to me like that. It's dead. Does it mean the dead are trying to communicate with me, trying to help me? And are not the dead, the spirits? The ancestors? And according to many of the Fairy-Faith (Evans-Wentz, 1966), the faery folk thems'elves?

But what should I do about it? It occurs to me that perhaps I should make an offering to the ancestors. When I ask the Secret Dakini Oracle about this, I get the card "The Way Through" (Douglas, Slinger, 1979. p. 70), which I take to indicate that this is indeed the way. But the question then becomes, what should I offer them?

So I return to the Celtic Oracles (Anderson, 1998) and I draw number 30 called Fairy Wind that speaks of "Invoking Exchange with the Spirit World" (p. 111). It says "... it is honorable to return a measure of your resources to it [the spirit world]". (p. 113). This strikes me as being particularly relevant because it again confirms the idea that I need to make an offering to the spirits/ancestors. But what should the offering be? Perhaps a hint is contained in subtitle of the Fairy Wind, which is *invoking*. Invocation is a magical practice (Bardon, 1975). It is paired with evocation, just as introvert is paired with extravert and functions in the same way. Evocation is the calling of spirits to manifest outwardly, and invocation is the calling of spirits to manifest within.

For example, the typical image of evocation is found in movies and books when a magician standing in a circle calls a spirit who appears before him to receive his (the magician's) orders and do his bidding. Invocation is most commonly seen in the practice of Voudoun (Metraux, 1972/1959; Deren, 1953), commonly called Voodoo, where the supplicants allow the god or spirit to temporarily indwell within them using them as a "horse" (Metraux, 1972/1959, p. 141). In terms of Depth Psychology, we are talking about purposely arousing communication with the Collective Unconscious, the inherited store of psychological information that has been transmitted through the generations within the genetic code.

In its lowest form, we are talking of a form of possession in which a demonic force takes over the individual. But here we are speaking of a higher form in which the individual is merged with something greater, as a poet or artist is taken over by the passion of their vision. They are taken over, in a sense, but are still thems'elves. They are possessed by the inspiration of their muse, their ally, their daimon. In religious devotion, this process is similar to someone inviting Jesus into their heart. And we can compare invocation to the transformation that an individual undergoes when they are filled with the numinous that is experienced as a personal revelation (Corbett, 1996).

Curiously, just after drawing the Celtic Oracle, I receive three cards at random from the Druid Animal Oracle (Carr-Gomm, 1994), the Hawk, which speaks of connecting to one's ancestral roots, the Sow, which speaks of giving generously, and the Owl, which speaks of developing sensitivity to the Otherworld. This seems to be further confirmation of what I've already

136

realized, I must do a ritual, making an offering to the ancestors, and inviting them to come alive within me.

Offerings to the Ancestors

I wait several days for the oracles to be auspicious. In the meantime, I compose enchantments in the form of rhymes, as the ancient Druids and Bards of the Celts did (Graves, 1966). When the time seems right, I proceed into my backyard, and beneath the large maple tree that lives there, and surrounded by a dozen other trees that I grow in pots, I invoke the ancestors.

These is a small table in my back yard and on it is a statue, about a foot and a half high, of a faerie sitting on a pedestal and holding a cupped flower in her hands. On this table I place a candle, which I light, and the other implements of my ritual, a small cigar, made from the tobacco I've grown mys'elf, a braid of sweet grass that was given to me for my birthday by an elf sister named Sarazan who said it contained blessings, a bottle of raspberry spritzer, and a vitamin bottle that has been sitting on my magic table for the last year filled with tobacco in water.

First I inscribe a circle on the ground in my imagination, saying:

Upon the Earth in other world
a circle I inscribe
and banish all dark forces
that from the light do hide
There's not a step that they can take
Not even to draw near
the outer line's enchantments
whose purpose is so clear,

137

I call now on my ancestors
of body, mind and soul
and of the spirit sacred
that have my life made whole.
I summon you and welcome bid
you come and join me now
and trust you'll lay your boon on me
all you can allow.
But this is not the reason
I've called you here today
but to give you many offerings
and to you my thanks display.
For you have ever guided me
come through in times of need
and from unhappy circumstance
you've ever had me freed.
So now this smoke most holy
I offer up to you.

Here, I light the cigar and begin smoking it, not by inhaling but by blowing the smoke outwardly through the cigar and offering it in the four directions, starting with the east, to the ancestral spirits of my kind. Then I say,

And by these waters sacred
our kindred I renew.

And now I open the bottle containing the tobacco water, and I pour it forth upon the ground in the four directions, this time beginning in the south. And having done so I continue, saying,

And I invite you now to live within
My body and my heart
that all the magics we've evoked
fulfilled they will now start.

Here I take the braid of sweet grass filled with blessings, and I place the end in the candle flame letting the smoke release the blessings and calling for the healing of the Earth and all those upon it.

It's at this point that I notice them. There is a radiance all across the hill that slopes upward directly behind the fence that limits my yard. And as I gaze at the radiance it seems in my mind's eye as though there are thousands of elves and pixies and myriad folk of the faerie world, seated there, their legs draw up to their chests, packed like an auditorium that is standing room only. As far as the eye can see, all along the hill from one end to the other, from top to bottom, seated on the hillside, sitting on tree branches, they're watching.

While I see all this in my mind, and surely no one else standing there would have seen it, this is not a fantasy or Active Imagination. I have not consciously set out to imagine this, but rather, I experience it as an event that I feel, more than anything. This is what has been called the felt vision (Raff, 1997a). It is a psychic vision. For while I see these faerie folk, in shadows outlined by radiance, even more I can feel them, feel them watching expectantly. And despite my surprise, I remain aware of the rite that I'm performing and continue, intoning:

And by the powers Faerie
And by the Elfin host
I raise this chalice magic
to all of you I toast.

And opening the bottle of spritzer, I pour it out to the spirits in the four directions, beginning in the west, where the elves are assembled on the hill. I save some for mys'elf pouring it into my sacred chalice, a one of a kind goblet, black with pink spots on it, that was handmade by a potter in Santa Cruz. I raise the chalice and offer toasts for luck and blessings to my ancestors, all who are now assembled before me, and to the powers of Faerie. I hear a sound in the maple tree looming over me, and I look up and know that at least one of them is peering down from there. Then I take what is left in the bottle and pour it in a circle, starting with the north, upon the earth and proceed by saying:

Now thanking you again, I say
with blessings, love, go on your way
but come again most soon I pray
or if it be your will do stay
we will in celebration play
Thanks again, I bid you well
The circle's opened by this spell.

And I look up from reading and they're gone. The hill is empty, although I can still feel them, just on the other side of the fence, hiding in shadows of the trees, but nowhere to be seen. Gathering up my tools, I go back inside, returning each magical tool to its proper place.

140

I gather three more bottles of sacred tobacco water, or spirit water, as I sometimes call it, for it is both food and attractant for the spirits. Remember what the shamans say about tobacco being the grandchild of the spirit world (Narby, 1998)? Well, we elves say if you want to attract the grandparents, dangle the grandchildren.

It is my intention now to go to the far reaches of my realm, Eldafaryn, and pour spirit water on the gateways, one to the south and one to the north, that are the entrances from Faerie into my world. In this way, they will be revitalized and blessed with spirit energy. I go southward first to the park that is at the end of my street. There are rocks there, placed like a dolmen, two upright stones with a capstone upon them, about three feet high, creating a passageway beneath and between. Here I pour the first bottle of spirit water, calling to the spirits and speaking to the surrounding trees. Just up from where I stand is the southern end of the hill behind my house, and there now I can see the radiance. I cannot make out their figures, but I know many of them are gathered there, still watching.

Having done that, I head north toward Nathandyryn, greeting the trees as I pass. There is one particular tree that stands at the center of my realm, whose golden leaves celebrate the summer, and with whom I have a special relationship. Although it is a chill winter night now and its leaves are long shed, among its branches you can see the mistletoe that was consider so sacred by the ancient Druids (Murray, 1988). Here I pour the second bottle of spirit water.

Proceeding to the north, I cross the street to the field that is the beginning of Nathandyryn. There are two tall evergreens that stand close together on the border of that realm and mine, and here I pour the third bottle, for this is the entrance from the north. The night has been quiet thus far, and except for a couple walking their dog, I've seen no one about. But here on the street the traffic begins whizzing by in both directions, and I decide to retreat, slipping into the dark, on a hidden

141

passageway that parallels the creek that is the eastern border of my realm. I greet the old willow who guards this passage as I pass. I can feel the spirits around me, but cannot see them now except in an occasional flitting of light in the corner of my eye.

Soon, I am near the south end of the park again, but to the southeast rather than southwest, where I begin. There are three ancient oaks here, a family who rule this part of my domain, and before them someone has situated two large boulders, about four feet high. Suddenly, I recall similar stones that I encountered on Waikiki Beach, in Hawaii. The ancient shamans of Polynesia sailed to the island of O'ahu in the far distant past and charged these stones to create healing and prosperity there.

When we were in Hawaii last summer (the summer of 2004), we stood before these stones, honoring them and the shamans who energized them. (Currently, a decade later, we live just a few streets from these stones and visit them frequently.) And now, thinking about those stones, while standing before the stones in my realm, I draw the energy from the ones in Hawaii and use it to energize the ones here, like a fiery match being brought to touch an unlit one. I can feel the stones healing the earth, radiating from the heart of Eldafaryn and spreading outward, bringing healing to all it touches. And now my task completed, I return home.

The Wreath

Our housemate had bought a wreath for Yule that we placed upon our front door. However now, two weeks into the new year, it is drying and the pine leaves litter the floor of the hallway every time we open the door. The next morning Silver Flame mentions this fact, and then says, "I think I'll put it in the backyard."

Now, this seems a sign to me, but of precisely what I'm not sure. Wreaths are used to decorate for the Yule season, they are used as crowns at times to celebrate heroes and their victories, but they are also used at funerals to honor the dead. Since I had just done a ritual honoring the dead in my backyard, her spontaneous placing of the wreath there the next morning, now that it is dying, seems somehow a confirmation of the magic.

However, in keeping with the course of this magic, I once again throw the coins to receive one of the Celtic Oracles (Anderson, 1998), this time getting number 62, which is called Treasures and speaks of the "Challenges of Mastery and Power" (p. 210). The treasures of which it speaks are the four treasures of the Tuatha De Danann, who were the Sidhe or Faerie Folk that came to Ireland (Gardner, 2003; MacManus, 1944) in ancient times bringing the treasures with them. The four treasures are "...the Stone of Fal, which shrieks when the rightful king sits upon it, the Spear of Lugh, which grants victory, the Sword of Nuada, from which no one escapes, and the Cauldron of the Daghdha, from which none leave hungry" (p. 210).

In other words, these represent the powers of greatness, authority and perhaps charisma, which would be the power of the rightful king who sits upon the stone; the powers of victory or success and accomplishment, the spear; the powers of the sword, which are protection and justice; and the powers of the cauldron, which are abundance and generosity. Everything it takes to establish, protect and nurture a people, a culture.

Surely this is a good sign. I called to the ancestors, and I am told of the ancient treasures of our people. And there are intimations of power and mastery. But what does this mean? The oracle makes clear that these powers will be challenged. It also says, "... your present circumstances require the right use of power" (Anderson, 1998, p. 211). So am I now to use these powers? And if so, how?

To get further clarification and perhaps a hint about what to do I throw the coins again and receive number 26, Rowan, the

Mountain Ash, which Anderson (1998) calls "The Alchemical Wand" (p. 98). It says, "A rowan branch above the door protects the home from unwanted intruders, especially mischievous spirits" (p. 98). It appears I am being offered the protection of the spirits, both from malignant spirits and also from harm in the "middle world" (p. 98), the world of man.

I decide to accept this protection, and perhaps guidance, and would put a branch of rowan above my doorways to symbolize that acceptance. However, here we have a snag. The rowan or mountain ash is a European tree, and while it has American relatives, they are all to be found in the northern climes close to and in Canada (Grimm, 1957).

However, there is a principle in magic called *like produces like*, which has been used by shamans from ancient times to the present (Frazer, 1951/1922; Harner, 1982), in other words, sympathetic magic. Just outside my home along the wall just before the doorway grows a Pyracantha bush, which, like the Rowan, produces bright red berries in the winter and whose leaves, while not exact, are very similar, sharing the same lance-like shape.

Blowing tobacco into the air, as an offering to the spirits, I cut three small branches from this bush, thank it and place them over the entrances to our dwelling, thus acknowledging my acceptance of the spirits protection. But once again, I am left to wonder, where do I go from here?

I find a hint further on in the rowan text that speaks of chthonic forces arising within me. It says, "In the slow steady pace of the underworld, you may be dreaming or "seeing" in new ways, prompted by otherworldly forces stirring within your unconscious mind." (Anderson, 1998, p. 100). It seems to me that what it is saying is, once again, I must be patient and wait, allowing the spirits I've invoked to have time to awaken within me.

This is not easy because I'm still in a fever to work on my thesis while I have the time to do so, but what can I do? I can't push

144

the river. But perhaps in the meantime, I can visit Enderea, my wise elven sister of Nathandyryn, and discover what she has to say on these things.

Discussion with Enderea 1-18-05, Active Imagination

I enter Nathandyryn near red headed Enderea's and walk to her tree house. I see lights beaming from her place and enter her tree at its roots and climb the spiral staircase that winds upward from within. I call out when I come to her entranceway (she doesn't really have a door but just a curtain that covers it), and she answers me saying, "Come in," and I enter.

"Oh, hello," she says, her cheeks lifting into a smile.

"I thought we might talk," I tell her.

"Of course," says she and waves me toward the pad on the floor that serves as her couch. I go and sit down and she asks, "Tea?"

"Please," I reply.

She says, "Just a moment," and then moves a screen away to reveal a small kitchen. She ignites a fire in what appears to be a stove of some sort and places a teakettle upon it. Then she comes and sits beside me. "So," she says, "any particular topic?"

"I'm not sure," I reply. "I mean I feel I need to talk to someone but find mys'elf at a loss for words as to what."

She smiles just slightly and says, "What is it, my love?"

"I just feel so hopeless at times."

"Yes?" She says, "How so?"

"I can never seem to find my place in the world out there. I mean, I survive, but I never really seem to succeed at anything. At least, nothing that will provide me with any security."

"And that's what you want? Security?"

"I wouldn't mind," I replied, "I mean I realize it's all an illusion and could all be swept away in an instant for anyone, yet, sometimes I think I wouldn't mind having some of that illusion. For the last thirty some years I've lived on luck and magic and the grace of the spirits. And I wonder when it will run out."

At this point the kettle begins whistling, and she rises to fix our tea.

"These I take it are not new considerations," she says over her shoulder.

"No, not new. Ancient and forever," I reply with a sigh. "I just get tired of living on the edge sometimes. I mean I could never trade it for a normal life, which is why I suppose I am always living on the edge. But..."

"You wish your magic was stronger?" She proffers.

"Exactly," I reply. "It's as though I've reached a barrier I can never seem to quite get through. It's as if there's some magic I'm missing. Perhaps some karma I can never quite expiate."

"And you want more?"

"Yes, more," I say, "Not just for mys'elf but for others as well. A better world. A better life. More love. I'm always saddened by my inability to cross social distances. I always feel that people should just instantly like me and be my friend."

"I agree. They should," she says, now bringing the tea and sitting beside me. "And one of the signs that the world is indeed mad is how difficult it is to ever get close to anyone out there."

"But what can I do about it?" I ask.

146

"What indeed," she replies. "You can't force them to like you. That would be ill magics, as you know. You can't contravene their wills or their destinies, but you're an enchanter and you can enchant them. Anything you can achieve willingly from them is fair game as long as you're keeping their interests in mind as well as your own."

"Well, my enchantments are pretty piss poor, if you ask me."

"Well, I didn't ask you, and for your information you have me totally enchanted. Besides you tend to grow on people. You slip up on them unawares. First they distrust you, and the next thing they know they realize you're one of the few people in the world they really can trust."

"Well, it doesn't seem to pay much."

"Is that what you want? Money?"

"Wouldn't mind," I say.

"You don't seem to put much effort toward it," she points out.

"That's the part I mind," I reply, and she laughs. "I still have this hunger to do something important. Something worthwhile, something that helps."

"And you don't think you do that?"

"I try." I stop and think, sipping my tea meditatively.

"And if you could do anything you wanted? Had all the money you needed, etc., what would you do?"

"If I had my dream, I'd have a huge Victorian house filled with elves or eccentrics, which are the same thing as far as I'm concerned, and I'd help them each develop their own particular talents, whatever it happened to be."

"A good vision," she agreed. "What's stopping you?"

"I seem to lack the money and don't know how to get it. In fact, I barely seem to get by month by month and never know when it will all fall apart. Of course, if I had charisma, I could get the money, but I seem to lack that as well. I suppose I could work like a maniac until I got it, but I've never been very good at that, and I seem destined to have jobs that keep me forever on the edge. Besides, I want to do it by magic. I just don't seem to have the power it takes."

"So we've come full circle."

"So it seems, and I conclude that for some reason it just isn't meant to be. At least at this time."

"You know what I think?" She offered.

"Please tell me."

"I think you frighten people a bit."

"So it seems."

"And you know why?"

"I'd love to," I reply.

"Because you're touched by Faerie. Because when most folks get near you they begin to sense that the magic just might be real, and magic scares them. Because it means all that they've assumed about the world is wrong, and that's just plain terrifying for most people."

"And what can I do about it?"

"Nothing," she said smiling and she stroked my left cheek. "Nothing but be yours'elf. You are meant to be who you are; and remember, you creep up on them. One of these days..."

"One of these lifetimes," I interject.

"Perhaps," she replies. "Certainly sometime, all the magics you have so carefully woven will fall into place."

"And then what?"

"You tell me."

"Then the world will be a far better place for all of us to live in."

"Exactly."

"And everyone will be free to be who they truly are."

"Yes."

"Even more, everyone will be nurtured and encouraged to become the best they can be in their own unique way."

"Precisely,"

"And in the meantime?" I ask, "And I do mean meantime."

"You do your magics."

"And if I fail?"

"Oh, my beloved," she said drawing my head to her and kissing me, "You can't fail. You're body may die in that world. It surely will. You may suffer. I trust not, however. And you have all of us looking after you. But the one thing that will not happen, is that you would fail."

"And why is that?"

"Because your vision is of the future. A future that will, sooner or later, come to be. By the way, I enjoyed your offerings to the ancestors the other night."

"You were there?" I ask, a bit surprised.

"Who wasn't?" she replies. "It was nice. Simple, sincere and to the point. Very effective in my opinion."

"But I haven't felt a thing," I say.

"And what were you expecting?" she asks.

"I don't know. Something. Something to rise within."

"And what have you felt?" she asks.

"I don't know. Quiet, I suppose. Peaceful. Perhaps a little sad for the world."

She lifts her eyebrows at this and peers at me intently. "Give it time, my love. Our magics are subtle magics. They don't force or violate. They don't compel. They enchant. But though they take longer to be fulfilled, they are the more lasting."

We are quiet for sometime, just sitting together. Then she says, "Why don't you go home now and give it time to settle in you.

You'll see. It will all come about in due course. I promise you."
And she takes my face in both her hands and kisses me again.
"Here," she says, "I'll walk you to the gateway." And she does.

Earth Rhythms

So I returned to the *Celtic Oracles* (Anderson, 1998) and receive
number 40, the Chambers of the Earth, which speaks of the
rhythms of the Otherworld and says, "For now, do not be
concerned if you feel that things are going too slowly" (p.145).
It is an accurate reply, if not quite the one for which I have
been hoping. Again, I'm confronted with the fact that nature
and the magic move at their own pace; and there is little I can
do but achieve patience.

However, number 40 also says, "Having drawn this oracle, you
may feel that a particular quality needs to be solidified to
become a more permanent part of your nature. If so, inquire of
the oracles once again" (p. 145). I do feel a particular quality
needs to a more permanent part of my nature, although I am
not quite sure what that quality is. Perhaps inquiring of the
oracles again will give me some hint about that aspect of being.

This time I receive number 42 which is entitled Changeling
(Anderson, 1998) and refers to "Otherworldly Knowing and
Talent" (p. 149). It says, "There are people... who naturally
convey supernatural qualities and often impress others as fey,
strange, mysterious, or extraordinary" (p. 150). My first reaction
to this is that they are, quite remarkably, describing me. I am,
without a doubt in my own mind, one of those people. Is my
talent the ability to contact that other world? Is my ability in
truth shamanism, a profession that has long been held in such
disregard that there are few left who are even able to nurture
such abilities? Am I, indeed, just as I have long suspected? To
check this assumption, I turn to another oracle.

This time I throw the cards of the Secret Dakini Oracle (Douglas, N., Slinger, P., 1979). and receive number 26 called Mean and Heavy which signifies the ability to take powerful action for the cause of what is right. However, it also says it refers to, "...the position of evolutionary responsibility through the communication of the unconscious and conscious parts of the Universal Mind," (p. 104). In putting these two ideas together, I come up with the image of someone who has the power to create communication between the conscious and the unconscious. To Jung, this is the process of Individuation. To the ancients, this is realm of the magician and the shaman.

Hints

In the meantime, the I Ching and the other oracles continue to tell me to be patient. There are small suggestions that things might be moving soon or that I may see small shifts in the mystic atmosphere. However, I'm continually warned not to expect too much at this point.

And indeed there are small signs, nothing decisive, yet enough to alert me to the possibility that something is taking place. My daughter gives me two pieces of agate shaped like a crescent moon and five-pointed star that she bought in Maui, both of which we still have and keep on our magic table. Does this have meaning? For some reason I get a mild numinous reaction upon receiving them. The moon is associated with the feminine mysteries, with witchcraft (Adler, 1979) and with enchantment, and stars are often associated with elfin enchantment. A few days later, I receive an email from someone across the country asking me if I have some idea of what a birthmark shaped like a five pointed star and a crescent moon might mean. This is surely a curious synchronicity, with no definite meaning but a sense of resonance. As though it is saying, things are beginning to attune.

151

Then, late that night I'm lying in bed when I hear our housemate and fellow member of our cohort in the Depth Program, Carol, call out, "There's a face on my wall." Silver Flame, my wife, goes to investigate and finds a candle Carol has been burning has cast an image of a face on her wall. I don't even bother to get up and look, but then I hear Carol say, "It's one of the ancestors." That's when I pay attention. The ancestors have given me a sign.

And the next evening I see a spirit out of the corner of my eye. It zips across the living room floor, a small dark grayish shape. I barely pay attention to it until about a half hour later I see it pass by me, climbing across the wall. This time I get a better look, and I realize it's our gargoyle.

We have a gargoyle, about two feet tall made of rubber (but made to appear to be stone) that sits atop our refrigerator. We call him Gargy (see figure 3, page 221). Remember that in an animistic worldview, everything biological is alive and has soul and all those things that we might call synthetic, such as swords, houses or statues, are capable of housing spirits. Thus the statue of Gargy is the home or body of a gargoyle spirit that protects our house. Since I have just recently placed the pyracantha over the doorways, it makes sense to me that he has been activated.

These are small things, but signs I think nonetheless. Small stirrings of the magic, like a breeze that comes along and rustles only a single leaf in a pile, then later stirs another. Something's moving but very slowly.

Body Magic

And there is something else. My body starts doing magic. While my mind is busy analyzing, arguing, fantasizing, etc. I notice my body simply is doing magic. It seals the entrances with wards, that is to say barriers to ward off evil. It pours blessings through the burning candles upon an ailing world. While I search inwardly for calm and composure, watching my mind chitter away, waiting for it to exhaust itself and come finally to silence, my body channels my feelings outwardly willing healing upon the earth and its inhabitants.

This is not the first time I have encountered this phenomenon. Often when I cast enchantments I find that my mind is engaged in a struggle between scientific skepticism and my own intent to accomplish the magic, somehow wishing to believe but not believing. However, my body has no doubts at all. I am drawn to do magic. I feel better when doing it. While my mind debates, I focus my attention on my body that acts without doubt or hesitation. The mind begins to be like a radio playing in the background that I can hear but to which I am no longer paying any attention. It is though I am acting out of muscle memory; only this is magical, psychic muscle memory, the memory of previous lifetimes, the memory of magical and spiritual training.

More Signs

Our housemate came home a little bit freaked out last night. She had gone out to dinner with a friend and told us that from the moment she had entered her car, it felt strange, as though there was an invisible presence. On the way to meet her friend she tells us she saw another creature, much like a gargoyle, float across the road and disappear under the van driving ahead of her. She related this to a television show (Dead Like Me) she had been watching in which creatures of that sort arrange accidents for those who are destined to die at a particular time. Naturally, she felt uneasy about this. But we pointed out to her that the creature disappeared into the car ahead of her and that what she had been feeling in her car was most likely one of

153

Gargy's assistants, for we have many gargoyles and other wards about our house, who had been sent to protect her. Still, it strikes me as significant that she actually saw the being with her eyes. She didn't imagine it or fantasize it; it was psychic seeing.

And today, 1 - 26 - 05, a complete stranger approaches me in the grocery store, says he's seen me about for years and asks me what I do. Now, it's only fair to say that I typically dress in a fashion that calls to mind the instructors of magic at Hogwarts. And surely this had something to do with his attraction. However, when my wife Silver Flame tells him we are elves, he begins to tell me about how he heard the elves laughing and giggling when he arrived home the other night. He assures me that he has really heard them and had not been imagining it. The spirits are beginning to manifest, or perhaps, because of the magic we have done, we, and those around us, are beginning to more readily see them.

The Birds

Last night I had a dream. I have walked out of my house (my house in the dream not my real house) and notice some mosquitos and gnats and other pests around and think that I will have to be careful of them. At that very moment, a huge column of birds drops from the sky, swoops down on the insects and begins eating them. The column is about six feet in diameter and so long that the head of the column circles the entire house before coming upon the tail, with which it then meets and merges, so there is a continuous circle of birds flying around the house.

Then, somehow I am seated in the driver's seat of a car with the door open, and as some of the birds fly by they swoop down on me and caress my face and hands with their feathers, barely brushing me as they pass.

There are several things I find interesting about this dream. First, the pests appear outside our house, and just a week ago I placed the pyracantha for protection about our house. Birds are often associated with spiritual forces, which is why in popular iconography angels have bird wings, while faeries have butterfly and dragonfly wings. So we could say that birds represent angelic forces. But who are the pests?

The pests in this dream are mosquitos and gnats. In an animistic worldview, dragonflies and butterflies are faeries. Faeries are not small humans with wings; that is, to the minds of these elves, but a sort of metaphor. Dragonflies and butterflies *are* faeries. They are alive. They have souls. They have spirits. They have their own intelligence and purposes. They are faery folk, just as birds, in an animistic worldview, are not representations of spiritual beings. They are spirits. But who are the gnats and mosquitos?

There is a form of faerie life called the Unseelie Court, which "... is the name given in Scotland to the wicked fairies who do all they can to hurt, frighten and destroy human mortals" (Briggs, 1979, p. 151). If the gnats and mosquitos are fairies, they surely are Unseelie faeries, determined to pester and prey upon me, those very dark spirits that the oracles warned me about while suggesting that I put the rowan/pyracantha about my dwelling. The fact that the birds go totally around my house would seem to indicate a thorough protection. But why are they caressing me?

I take the fact that they are caressing me as a good sign. It is intimate, in its way. It connotes friendship and relationship. They are not protecting me because I have compelled them to do so but because of the affection they hold for me. Yet why am I seated in a car?

Does this indicate that their protection extends to my travels as well? That is to be hoped but is by no means certain. However, what is clear to me is that now I need to return to the Celtic Oracles.

The Faery Lover

Throwing the coins again I receive number 48 entitled the Faery Lover (Anderson, 1998) whose theme is "sensuality" (p. 168). The notion of a mystical union of marriage between the spirits, gods and those in human incarnation is not a new one. When I was at military school as a boy, I served variously as an altar boy, acolyte and incense censer carrier at various masses and other ceremonies, including a couple of times when the archbishop came and performed the rites of marriage for the young novitiate nuns taking their vows and becoming the brides of Christ.

Voodoo/Voudoun also has the idea of this "mystical marriage" (Metraux, 1972/1959, p. 212) in which the devotee marries the spirit or god. However, unlike Catholicism where the brides of Christ are bonded in an exclusive relationship with their god, in Voudoun the mystical marriage does not prevent a more mundane marriage as well.

Such connections between the faery folk and mortal humans is a common theme of faery lore, although with a less religious and more romantic, yet equally magical, aspects. It can be seen in Spenser's *Fairy Queen* (Keightley, 1978/ 1880), the tales of *Tam Lin* (Ipcar, 1973) or Tamlane (Briggs, 1967) and *Thomas the Rhymer* (Briggs, 1978) all variations of the same tale.

Two things occur that highlight the significance of receiving this oracle. First, I had a dream the very night I received the Faery Lover in which I'm riding on a train with a co-worker who begins to make out with me. I wake up as I begin to fondle her breast. Having this dream immediately after receiving the oracle is significant to me. Metraux (1972/1959) writes that "Spirits are apt to communicate with the faithful by means of dreams" (p. 143). In Voudoun lore, this would have been seen as a visitation of the goddess Erzulie who is the goddess of love (Deren, 1953). In this case, I will simply call her the Faery Lover and acknowledge it as a confirmation of the Faery Lover oracle.

The other thing that occurred happened earlier in the day, before I drew the oracle. I was shopping at a local health food store and encountered an acquaintance that works there. She was in the process of putting up displays and decorations for Valentine's Day. As I engaged her in a light banter about the holiday, she revealed to me that, though she is a very attractive woman in my opinion, she had no romance in her life of late. In fact, she said, she hadn't even had a date in ages.

Now the reason I relate this second, even though it occurred first, is that it was only after receiving the oracle and the dream that I paid great heed to this encounter. I decided then, as an act of kindness and friendship to create an enchantment for her so that she could attract a suitable companion.

I created a glyph that has two hearts with eyes and ears and lips, with the lips touching in a kiss. On each of the hearts the pointed end has been elongated into a tail which are entwined like the snakes of the caduceus wand, one ending in an arrowhead, like the symbol for Mars or the masculine sign and the other in a cross as in the sign for Venus or the feminine. I place this glyph (see figure 4, page 222) on a sheet of paper with instructions for burning a red candle that I've included with it and the following enchantment:

A lover true shall come to me

whose presence will my heart set free

And now this sweetheart will arrive

Begins a love that long survives

And as our hearts do intertwine

I know this lover true is mine.

After burning the candle, place this enchantment on your altar or carry it with you.

It is a beacon that will attract your true love.

To empower this spell I go within my portable magic circle (see figure 5, page 223), which is painted on an old circular tablecloth with fringe about its outer circumference. I burn a red candle like the one that will be included with the spell, and I offer the sacred tobacco to the spirits. Then I recite the following enchantment:

Faery Lover, listen well
and smile upon this loving spell
so those who chant it soon will find
their will fulfilled in ample time
their hearts be healed, their souls revived
their bodies tingling and alive
their spirits wakened and renewed
their minds clear sighted, focused, true
And all the love that they do need
will start to grow with this spell's seed.

Placing the candle on the paper, I drip water on it from a bottle that I've had for over a decade that bears the label Greater Love. I allow the water to drip from the candle and be absorbed into the paper. Next I anoint the candle with a perfume oil called Lover's Moon and roll the candle so that the oil once more is transferred to the paper which holds the enchantment. Having done all that I thank the spirit of the Faery Lover and depart the circle. All that's left to do is deliver the enchantment.

The Faery Lover Returns

That night I have another dream. I'm walking on a train accompanied by a beautiful woman wearing a brightly decorated brocade coat. We are moving through the train from car to car heading toward the front. She stops me and kisses me and I awake. This dream is in many ways, nearly identical to the precious dream. The woman has changed from someone I know to an unknown figure, and instead of sitting on the train we are walking within it. However, what strikes me particularly about this dream is the train itself. I barely noticed the train as an element of the first dream, but now that it has been repeated I see it to be an especially significant symbol. But what does it signify?

Again the goddess, the faery lover has come to me. And once again, it is surely a good sign regarding the enchantment I've created. But what is the message of the train? For surely, it is a message of some sort. First, I ask myself, why a train? Why not a jet, airplane, bus, or car? Certainly a train denotes movement and travel, but so do those others. So why a train and not the others?

Two things stand out in my mind about a train. First, unlike the others, it moves on tracks. Thus while it indicates movement, perhaps progress, it also seems to indicate very directed progress; perhaps we could say focused progress. There is no option with a train, you go forward, or backward, or stop, but you cannot deviate without disaster from the chosen course. Thus the train seems to be an indication of magic functioning within certain very strictly defined limitations.

The second idea that comes to me about a train, is its associative meaning, which is to say, to train or training. It seems to be an indication of a process of learning. Does the fact that we are walking within the train from back toward the front indicate a sort of progress within that training? And what is the training? Love? Enchantment? To the elfin mind they are

159

virtually the same thing. And so saying I decide to return to Nathandyryn to visit my faerie lovers who abide there.

Anathea and Adana 1- 28 - 05, Active Imagination

I'm strangely excited, like a child about to get on a roller coaster. I begin deep breathing to calm myself and enter a trance. Even as my breath deepens, however, I can still feel the inner surge of power and expectancy. I create my imaginal body, what is often called the astral body (Regardie, 1972), the subtle body (Raff, 2000), or the body of light (Butler, 1969), and step out of my seated form, move to the other side of the room and look back at myself. Then I go to the threshold that appears to normal eyes to be but a bookcase, and I step though to Nathandyryn, arriving just south of Alyryn's house.

I go to the creek that is the eastern boundary of this yard, passing between his house and his neighbor's, the poet that lives just to the south of him. I follow the creek up a ways to the small, very ornamentally carved and engraved footbridge that connects the two banks, and I cross over.

I come to the stairs that lead up to the platform that links Adana's and Anathea's tree houses, which each start on the same level about 20 feet up, but are built around separate trees. Arriving at the top I find the two of them seated and chatting on the far side of the platform. They glance my way and smile. They both rise, and Anathea says, "Shall I get you some tea?"

And I reply, "Please."

Then she flashes a smile at Adana and retreats into her tree house. Adana and I stand, about ten or twelve feet apart, gazing at each other.

160

"It's been a while, I know," I say. Is it an apology? An expression of remorse? I feel somewhat guilty for having been gone so long but am glad now to be here. But she just stares at me, and instead of replying crosses the space between us, slips her arms about me and whispers, "At last," almost like a sigh, draws me to her and kisses me full on the mouth. I won't go into the details here, but several minutes later, she pulls slightly away from me, looks into my eyes and says, "Hello, love," which is followed by more gratuitous kissing and fondling.

"Tea?" I hear Anathea say, and we glace over to see her approaching with a silver tray that bears three cups and a pot of tea. She places the tray on a small wooden table that rests near the trunk of her tree and comes over to us, extending upward on her tiptoes (as she is shorter than I) and gives me a quick kiss, saying, "Glad you've come." Then she goes and pours the tea.

Adana takes me by the hand and leads me to two cushions that are situated near the table. "I'll fetch another," she says and returns shortly from her house with a third cushion. "So, what brings you?" She asks as she settles on the cushion.

"You," I respond, "And you," indicating Anathea.

"Then you are most fortunate, sir elf, because you have found us both."

I find mys'elf at a lost for words. I laugh at mys'elf and shake my head, "I never know what to say."

Adana looks at me and says, "You think words are what I want from you."

"What do you wish from me?" I ask.

"Your presence, when possible. And if you would but think of me fondly from time to time, it would make my heart most glad."

"I always think of you fondly and quite often," I assure her.

161

"I think you lie," she says, but this is a sweet and teasing accusation, and she adds, "But it is a lie I am most eager to believe."

"It is no lie," I say. "I do think of you and all my friends and kindred of Nathandyryn. And more than that, I long for you at times, more than you realize."

"But not as much as I long for you," she responds.

"I don't know how to compare our longings," I say, "But I think that they might be equal and the same."

We pause and sit in silence, sipping our tea. She grins at me and gives me that sly look that her dark brown eyes get sometimes, and she says, "I love you, Zardoa."

"And I love you two, too," I reply.

"Ever the wit," she says.

"Ever witless," I say.

She seizes me by my hair with her left hand and says, "Never demean yours'elf to me, sir elf. I love you too much to listen to that." And she releases me, making a face as she does so that clearly states, pay heed.

"Anyone want biscuits?" Anathea asks and retreats to her house again, before either of us can answer.

"What magics have you been up to lately?" Adana asks me.

"What makes you think I've been up to any magics?" I ask, innocently.

"Hah!" She says, which is both a laugh and a comment. "As though you could not. I know you better than you realize. You live for magic. The only thing you find more interesting is sex, and if you can combine the two you're in heaven."

"Well, Elfin anyway," I say.

"So?" And she looks at me deeply, patiently waiting.

So I tell her of the small enchantment I created for my lonely friend.

162

"And you're not trying to get her for yours'elf?"

"No," I reply honestly. "It's strictly a gift. No strings attached."

"Not that I would mind, mind you," she says, mimicking me affectionately.

"It seems to me that doing something pure and unselfish is good for my soul every once and a while."

"It seems to me doing something sensual and mutually pleasurable is good for my soul quite often," she says.

"Wouldn't mind at all," I reply, and we kiss again, until Anathea returns with the biscuits.

"I see things are proceeding swimmingly," she comments.

Adana replies, "Like a school of dolphins."

"I didn't think dolphins went in schools," Anathea said, "That's fish. Dolphins are mammals."

"What do they go in?" Adana asks her.

"I don't know, riots, I think."

"I thought that was pixies?" Adana replies, then shrugs, turns back to me and says, "So what other magics have you been up to?"

"Feeding the spirits," I tell her. "Energizing the wards around my house. Calling up Faerie and encouraging it to spill into the mundane world."

"Nothing much then," she says, "Just the usual."

"More or less," I reply.

"We've been feeling it," Anathea tells me. "The world on the other side has been feeling very strange the past few years. Somebody's been calling up demons and feeding the dark gods the blood sacrifices they so hunger for."

"All the more reason and need to feed our own spirits with love, don't you think?" I say.

"Oh, yes," she replies. "But I'm not certain how much good we can do over there. They don't want us anymore. They'd rather bathe in blood and death than share their lives in love."

"So it seems," I reply thoughtfully. "Yet there are others, many, many others who would return to the ancient ways of nonviolence and loving. They just need encouragement. And right now, they need it a lot. It is so easy to get sucked into the passion and the hatred. And so hard at times to stand up for love and loving when it's so often projected as weakness, and when nudity is thought to be dirty, and violence somehow seen to be normal."

Anathea reaches across the table and takes my hand, giving it a supportive squeeze. "Don't worry," she says, "We're with you all the way."

"All the way," agrees Adana but then she grins and smirks and laughs. "I'm sorry," she says, "I don't mean to make light of it."

"Not at all," I tell her. "I agree with you. Lightness is exactly what is needed."

"Seriously though," she says, "Whatever magics you do we'll support. Won't we, Anathea?"

"All the way," says Anathea with a gleam in her eye, and we all three laugh.

"Thank you," I tell them. "I need, count on, and appreciate your support. And if there's anything I can do for you..."

"Well, now that you mention it," says Adana, and again we break up into laughter.

Changing the subject slightly, I say, "I keep discovering I don't take people seriously enough.

"Oh," says Anathea, "How so?"

"I just never quite appreciate how deeply wounded and therefore crazed they are from the pain, much to my regret at times. I keep vowing to take them more seriously."

Anathea nods and Adana comments, "They must need it somehow."

"Exactly," I say, "Somehow I fail to empower them if I don't take them seriously. But at the same time I can't help feeling that part of their problem is taking thems'elves so damn seriously."

"Quite a paradox," agrees Anathea, "But perhaps if you treat them with absolute deference and respect, they'll be able to lighten up on thems'elves."

"It is to be hoped anyway," I say. Then, "I wish I could heal people."

"I know," agreed Adana. "Don't we all. It would be nice to be able to just go up to anyone and heal whatever ails them."

"My thoughts precisely," I say.

"But then, we'd just be interfering with their own will and karma. Ultimately, they have to heal thems'elves. All we can do is offer them love, guidance and encouragement."

"The Elf Queen's Daughters used to tell me they saw their job as instilling people with confidence," I tell them.

"A worthy endeavor," Anathea agrees.

We pause again to sip our tea and snack on the biscuits, which are scone-like things sweetened with honey and filled with cherries, while we ponder all that had been said.

"So what next, elf lord?" asks Adana after a bit.

"Why do you call me that?"

"You know why. It's your responsibility," she replied.

"And your due," adds Anathea, flipping her head to get her long white hair out of her face; revealing, by doing so, her pointed ears.

"Well, I'm glad you think so," I say. "I don't feel like much of an elf lord most of the time," I confess.

"Perhaps," says Anathea, "But you always act like one and that's the important thing. Besides, that world tarnishes everything. Burnish any soul, peel away the layers of mud and the accumulations of dust and grit and you nearly always find something unique and precious underneath."

Again we fall silent; the birds are chirruping in the trees about us. The night is coming and it's getting cooler, but it's still warmer than it is on the other side. I feel a tremendous sense of contentment and acceptance being among them. And not just with them. The birds, the trees, the very air seems to embrace me and soothe my inner being. There is a haunting fragrance in the air, a little like cinnamon, and inhaling it makes me nearly want to swoon with the sensual pleasure of it. I sigh deeply.

"I want to transform that world," I tell them. "I want to transform it to be more like this one."

"A noble ambition," says Anathea. "But the dark gods won't like it."

"No, no they won't," I admit. "But then they've never cared much for me. I suppose I've been lucky that they think me so insignificant that they barely notice me."

"And you have your guardians and protectors. Never forget," Adana points out.

"And the problem with transforming that world is the same one as healing all you meet," adds Anathea, "You can't change them against their will, at least not for the better anyway."

"But how about those who are willing?" I ask. "There are many, many whose souls cry out for a better world. And what of me? Can I not transform my own world? Make it a realm unto itself, in a sense? A little bit of Elfin alive in the mundane world?"

"You have that," Anathea points out.

"But I hunger for more," I say.

"Then you must transform yours'elf, my dear love," says Adana. "Have you considered the possibility that the person you really need to take seriously is yours'elf? Sometime, sooner or later, you will have to quit dithering, quit doubting yours'elf and plunge utterly into the magic."

"There's no other way," says Anathea.

"Back to going all the way," I say.

"Exactly," says Adana, this time with no hint of humor. "You must commit yours'elf utterly. Rid yours'elf of all extraneous doubt, and do."

"And you will find, I think," says Anathea, "that the moment you do so the whole universe, and certainly all of Faerie, will turn its head and take notice of you."

"And magics you've only dreamed of so far, by which I mean luck unimaginable, will come to you like iron drawn to a magnet."

"You think?" I ask.

"We know," they say together.

And shortly there after, I return to Eldafaryn to ponder all that they have said to me. I feel enthused and excited and still filled with energy. I wait until the next day to do the oracles again, giving the experience time to settle within me.

The Choice

Throwing the coins I receive number 55, in the Celtic Oracles this time, it is called the Hammer God (Anderson, 1998) who bears the "Scepter of Authority and Choice" (p. 190). The choice seems clear enough in essence, since it was discussed in my conversation with Adana and Anathea. It is a choice to remain forever attached to the world as it is and change it from within, or to create a new world that is contiguous to, but independent of, the world of consensual reality. However, while it seems a simple choice in thinking about it, like so many things, it is easier said than done. For the choice is really one of consciousness and focus of attention. Do I spend much of my time thinking about the mundane world beyond my own concerns, filling my mind with political opinions, etc.? Or do I concentrate all my energy toward the vision with which I have been graced of a better world that could be and put all my energy and thoughts toward creating it? The oracles themselves urge me to wait, to make no hasty decision, but to ponder the possibilities for a while.

So I do so, allowing the choice to wash over me for several days, waiting to see if a dream might come to guide me and at the same time haunted by a vision I had while visiting Adana and Anathea of extending the wards around my space by placing pyracantha branches at the four entrances to my realm, or eald as I call it.

What Dreams May Come

This is but a dream fragment, but I am walking down a dirt path that is meandering through a tropical forest. As I move forward I can see the sea through the trees and in the distance the big island of Hawaii, and I realize I'm on one of the other islands. I become fearful, afraid that a volcano could erupt or the islands sink back into the sea. However, as I'm experiencing this fear a voice tells me that I am in paradise and should enjoy it to the fullest, that death comes when it will and that I need not bother mys'elf thinking about it.

The dream seems to confirm my intention of creating my own island of Elfin in the midst of the vast sea of consensual reality. And the urge to place the wards at the entrances to my realm is

168

growing within me. I speak to the pyracantha, telling it of my plan and asking its permission to cut a few more branches. Since I have on numerous occasions helped protect it from the trimming frenzy of the gardener that is sent each year, always persuading him to let them grow out as much as possible, I sense the pyracantha is glad to oblige. Beside, I tell it that I will not merely cut the branches and place them about but will push them into the moist soil so there is a chance these clippings will root.

Found Objects

To cut the branches, I use my magical knife. I call it magic both because it has been among the implements of my enchanter's trade for the last 20 years but also because, in the elven tradition, as well as others, found objects are magical (Elf Queen's Daughter, personal communication, 1975). Carlos Castaneda sorcerer's party, by which I mean those sorcerers who surrounded him after he became a famous author and not the sorcerer's party of Don Juan that he wrote about in his books, would scramble for money found on sidewalks, calling it magic money and saving it up for the purchase of magical tools (Wallace, 2003). Twenty years ago, I found the knife, which has a wooden handle that bears designs carved in the interwoven style of the ancient Celts, at a nature preserve called Anafyn or Annwyn, named after the Otherworld of the Celtic legend (Matthews, 1995). (For the full story of finding this knife see our book *Eldafaryn: True Tales of Magic from the Lives of the Silver Elves*.)

I use this knife to cut four branches from the pyracantha. Then I proceed into the street with them, with the idea of declaring my intention to the spirits while standing at the center of my realm. I intend to do this before proceeding to the openings to the mundane world, which are different from the gateways to the other world that I energized, opened and empowered earlier in this process. However, as I move into the street something catches my eye. It is a circular metal covering, which is itself surrounded by a circle of concrete that allows access to the sewer system.

This catches my attention for two reasons. First, it is a double circle, which is the traditional form of the magician's circle of ritual magic (Bardon, 1975). Second, it is connected to the sewage system, and it strikes me that if I am declaring the independence and sanctity of my realm that the very bottom, so to speak, is a good place to start. There is, however, one small catch.

The lid of the sewer is surely made of iron, either cast iron or steel, and in traditional fairy tales iron is poisonous to the faery folk, like kryptonite for Superman. I might for that reason avoid the use of this circle in my magic. Instead, I determine to use it to my advantage, for in the process of declaring my realm I will also be banishing wicked spirits from it, and I announce this as I step within the circle. As I go about planting the pyracantha they will thus be given a chance to exit my realm, once it is sealed, however, they will have to bear the responsibility for the suffering they will encounter if they remain.

I walk toward the entrance to the street, cross the road and plant the first branch just within the boundary of Nathandyryn, linking our realms. I place the branch at the very center of the dead-end road that leads into our street. However, I have also, by placing it on the far side of the road, included the road that passes by our street, within our domain, allowing a right of way to those passing by, but preventing ill spirits from entering our demesne. This opening is to the north.

I now proceed to the northeast corner of our eald where there is a seldom-used walkway that runs by the creek that is our eastern boundary. Here I place the second branch, sealing the entrance from injurious forces. Then, as I turn toward the south and the entrance that awaits there, I begin to hear them.

I do not see them, mind you. They will not show themselves to me, but I can hear them chattering in my mind, little demons doing their best to disturb my concentration and prevent me from carrying out my intention. First, they try fear. What if the police find me walking about in my black coat that looks like a sorcerer's robe? I ignore them and keep walking. Then they try arousing my insecurities. This is really meaningless, you know, it's not like you really have any power and any of this makes any difference. I continue on ignoring these demons. Whether we see them as internal, as my own random thoughts and paranoia, or external, actual spirits whispering in my mind, matters little. The I Ching (Wilhelm, 1967) says, "... we should not combat our own faults directly. As long as we wrestle with them, they continue victorious." (p. 167). It counsels that the best way to deal with evil either within or without us is to make determined progress toward the good. So I continue on.

Perceiving my determination, their voices become less and less pronounced and gradually fade. They are leaving me, headed for the exits while that's still an option, mumbling imprecations (or imp-precations?) as they do so. For they wish to be gone before they are encircled by the pyracantha. Pyr, being from the word for fire and acantha from the Greek akantha meaning thorn (Soukhanov, 1984), thus fire thorn. They will be burned if they stay by fiery thorns or spears.

Then I come upon something I hadn't counted on. There is another entrance to my realm. I had forgotten about it because it is a gated bridge spanning the creek to the east, which is only unlocked during the daylight hours. I could go back for another branch, but decide against doing so as it would interrupt the circuit of my realm. Instead, I improvise, taking the smaller of the two branches left to me and planting it beside the bridge and then cutting the larger branch into two.

I find a small boulder near the south entrance and place the next branch there. I am nearly done with my rounds, but there is one entrance left. This path is in the southwest, directly opposite to the seldom used entrance to the northeast. It is a secret path that skirts through from the street above and was created by those who live up there as a shortcut to the park, even though signs proclaim *no trespassing* all along it.

Having planted the final branch I head back to my house, speaking to the trees, as I have been doing throughout my journey, telling them of my Quest.

Most people say,

"You only have one life to live."

Elves say.

"You only have one life to live at a time,

so do your best with each one,"

which is also how we approach relationships.

CHAPTER 7: CONCLUSION

> *"The magic people haven't been invited to attend the party..., for fear that they might dance. They haven't been invited to speak at the party, for fear that they might sing. They haven't been invited to run the party, for fear that they might change it.*
>
> *They would have, and now they're going to."*
> *(Williamson, 1997, p. 241)*

This Study

This study was a depth inquiry using primarily the processes of dream interpretation and active imagination within a framework of personal myth. My thesis is that the personal myth, when conscious and functional within normal reality is an effective means of integrating the unconscious and conscious elements of the psyche. I will now speak to the results and conclusions I have drawn as to the efficacy of that process.

Bodily Felt Sense

The first thing I notice in examining the findings and the result of my process work is what Gendlin (1986) calls the bodily felt sense. He uses this term in dream interpretation, but I am extending it here, as I extended other principles of dream interpretation, to my body's reaction to the overall process.

When I began the study, I was exhausted and felt emotionally and psychologically drained. I was doing the study immediately after an intense semester of work in the Depth Program and, because of time factors, having to carry on the study during my winter break. However, what is clear was that after the very first step into the realm of the personal myth, which was done to rejuvenate energetically, I was filled with energy. My body was electrified and I felt psychologically driven, and it took all my will power to establish composure and to proceed in a steady and measured way. All the time, I struggled with impatience, born of an urge to proceed as rapidly as possible. I felt rather like a child on Christmas morning, having to wait for his parents to have their coffee before being allowed to tear into the presents.

However, this was a brief study, taking place during a period of a little over a month, and I would question whether such an energy level would have continued if the study had been carried out over, say, a year's time. However, there is no question that for the limited period involved in the study the effect was dramatic.

Body Knowledge

I also observed that quite frequently during the study while my mind debated, doubted, questioned and quibbled, my body acted instinctually, carrying on the mythic acts on its own, as though my unconscious took over while my conscious mind chatted. It might have been absorbed in analyzing or overwhelmed with uncertainties and fears, scanning for potential routes of escape or excuses, but my body continued on, absolutely certain in its acts.

Anima

From a Jungian perspective, I think it is obvious that most of the characters that appeared in my active imaginations, were various forms of my anima, or my inner feminine, which form a link between the individual and collective consciousness (Jung, 1957/1934). They were contra-sexual figures, as Jung (1959c/1938) hypothesized they would be. I think the flirting and the undertone of sexual innuendo make the fact that these were anima figures quite definite. Furthermore, this erotic undertone is a common and traditional aspect of the shaman's relationship with his/her ally (Raff, 1997b).

What I did not see in my process was any form of shadow (Conger, 1988) figure, that aspect of the self that the conscious mind tends to deny and disassociate itself from, projecting it on to others in a negative form. Again, this lack of the appearance of the shadow I take to be due to the limited duration of the study (approximately one month), rather than the idea that I don't have a shadow.

The study did, however, reveal some of my complexes, most prominently in the form of fears and paranoia, which, within the magical world, are seen to be the demons actively attempting to keep the magic from happening. This seems to confirm Jung's (1960b/1946) belief that there are aspects of the unconscious that actively seek to disrupt and interfere with the integration of the psyché.

Those who know me well and know that Silver Flame and I have been together, sharing nearly every moment of our lives, for the last 27+ years, may wonder where she was in the Active Imagination process, and why I didn't include her in it. But Jung advised against ever taking Living Persons into the active imagination (Hannah, 2001). (I also extend that to include those who had been living previously.) In fantasy, one might imagine having a hot and torrid affair with Albert Einstein or Madame Curie, or a deep intellectual and spiritual discussion with Angelina Jolie or Brad Pitt, but Active Imagination as a process, if done according to the psychological guidelines, limits one's encounters to imaginal beings. Usually, as indicated above, they are seen as aspects of one's own psyché from a psychological viewpoint or of spirits of the nether realms from a shamanistic point of view. We leave the individual reader to decide how they will consider these beings. From my own point of view, my imaginal characters are in many ways all variations of Silver Flame, their kindness and lovingness toward me, all reflective of her own kind and compassionate soul.

I should note that while I continued doing Active Imagination for a while after this, I discontinued the process when we moved to Hawaii. At first I keep think about doing it, but I never did so. Instead, I continued to merge my personal myth with the world around me so I've become increasingly able to stand between the worlds and see the world of Faerie overlapping the world of consensual reality. Where other folks see normal, or not quite normal folks, walking down the street, I see faeries and gnomes and all manner of otherkin and elfin folk. This is in keeping with my increasing exploration and understand, however meager, of Quantum Reality. Cynthia Sue Larson in her book *Quantum Jumps* says, "For spiritually focused individuals, quantum jumping holds the promise of attaining an optimal state of lucid living awareness in which one becomes aware of living in a waking dream, while attaining an energized, grounded state of consciousness." (Larson, C., 2013). I'm living my dream.

Meaning

I must admit that the world as it exists, the world of consensual reality, often makes little sense to me. I find it hard to understand how people can be so violent and hateful toward each other, and my own life in the midst of that world seems without purpose. However, within the realm of my personal myth, my life takes on purpose and meaning. This may in part be because, while consensual reality deals with my life now, my personal myth encompasses the possibility of lifetimes of development. When seen from that perspective, when seen from the concept of evolutionary development of the soul and spirit, my life and my work become filled with meaning. And the result of that meaning is an energizing of my being. Where previously I felt drained by life and the world, I am now, due to the integration of my myth within the world, filled with enthusiasm and a sense of possibility. This seems to confirm what Bond (1993) and others theorized about the affect of integrating myth into one's life.

Dreams

It may also be noted that the dreams I had during this period of entering and living within my personal myth, reflected the movement or events of the myth at that time. This seems to be an indication both of the success of the personal myth and the magical acts as a means of communication with the unconscious and, I think, an indication that the psyché took the myth seriously. By living the myth, I was affecting my psyché.

Into the Woods

I also see an interesting parallel between my active imaginational process and the event of my childhood (The Forest Perilous) where I was lead into the forest by two little girls. It is true that my active imagination is more adult in nature, but the essential innocence is still there. In my opinion,

I am still being lead into the unknown by feminine characters who are nurturing, protecting and guiding me. This fact reinforces my conclusion of the powerful influence of the Anima in my psyché. But that is only to be expected. From my mother, to the nuns at military school, to the Elf Queen's Daughters, to Silver Flame, women have been a powerful influence in my life and continue to be so.

Individuation

I also note that the process of living the Personal Myth resulted in an affirmation of the myth itself. By that I mean that the progress of the Active Imaginations tended toward encouragement for becoming increasingly involved with my Personal Myth, that is more in tune with, and more involved with my personal understanding of myself apart from the world's view of me. The process seemed to encourage me to become more in touch with my own sense of s'elfhood.

Further Study

The suggestion that this study promotes is that by integrating one's personal life in the world and one's inner life of purpose, meaning and, yes, fantasy, an individual's ability to interact with the world is enhanced. One's personal energy is heightened, and because of this, one has more energy to direct toward creativity or other pursuits.

However, as denoted earlier, this was a very limited study and I think a proper study would require a year if not more to allow a full range of development and a full functioning of the various aspect of the psyché. The closest study to this one, whose

178

findings were similar and suggestive of the same results was Weeks (James, Weeks, 1996) study of eccentrics. However, Week's study did not directly view the life of the eccentric as a personal myth, although that was clearly the case in many of the stories cited, nor did it follow the life of an eccentric over a period of time. Hillman's (1997) study of the lives of exceptional individuals, although done in hindsight, is a more pervasive indication of the efficacy of this theory.

The Last Word

As a courtesy, I think I will allow the personal myth the final words of this part of the thesis. The myth speaks:

I don't dare tell you the truth, do I?

Or perhaps I do.

But what's the point for you will but turn your head away,

your ears already closed,

certain you already know it.

But somewhere out there, they listen.

The trees inclining branches,

the brooks ceasing to babble for a moment,

the clouds in respectful silence tiptoeing by,

and everywhere the creatures wild

and the places untamed

watch as rivers of starlight pour from my fingertips

and I weave a world not seen for thousands of years,

which men in their folly proclaim never existed

because they did not invent it.

While the birds sing to hear my song,
and the skies weep with joy,
and every wound is healed by my touch.
But I will not tell you any of this.
For you would not believe.
Instead I'll wait till you are half asleep
and stroke your head tenderly,
and sing a lullaby of awakening,
till dreams slip up on you
and the world you thought a mere fantasy,
born of my breath,
surrounds you.

If we elves were to compare ourselves to a food,
it would probably be dark chocolate,
though some might say pizza,
or coffee or Masala Chai,
or perhaps a rich smorgasbord of culinary delights.

CHAPTER 8:

FURTHER CONSIDERATIONS
CONCERNING LIVING ONE'S MYTH

"GIVE ME THE LAST CHANGE OF PERFECT BEING, WHEN I AND MY IMAGE ARE ONE."

(WAITE, 1974, PG. 165)

A Little Modesty Goes a Long Way

You will notice that while we proposed the idea that basing one's personal myth upon real events in one's life generally has more power for the individual than simply basing it on fantasy, we did not offer this as an absolute. The reason for this is, in part, that there are individuals who live almost totally in their fantasy worlds and do quite well and are energized and even happy to do so. Usually, however, these are children who have no real need, or any ambition at that point in their lives to succeed in the world, nor do they seek the acceptance or approval or even belief of others who do not share their myth. Quite often, their myth arises because they already have the nurturing and acceptance of loving parents, siblings or friends.

However, this is also the case with cults and other budding religions, who create their own fantasy, their own view of the world, their own small circle of consensual reality, that often comes into conflict with the existing religions and are persecuted for seeing the world differently, although some, in time, become one of the dominant belief systems. This is true of Christianity, Islam, and even Buddhism, which came into conflict with Taoism in China (see the folk tales concerning *Monkey* that, as a sub-theme, concern this conflict (Yu, 1977).). In part, the effort to establish one's personal myth is to make it viable in the world at large. Modern Wiccans are currently engaged in this struggle, the struggle not necessarily to have their views accepted but to have them respected.

Those who use their myth as a means of self-validation in the world seldom get what they so hunger to receive at first, even when their myth is based on quite real events, rather than pure fantasy. Budding Christianity, for instance, could not look to the world at large to validate it; rather it found itself persecuted. It had to prove itself. This is true of individuals as well.

We have in our lives, and we expect you have as well, encountered numerous individuals who make all sorts of ludicrous claims to powers and abilities, titles and positions of authority that are frequently derived from pure fantasy. There are also those who have very real accomplishments, such as being Philosophus in the Golden Dawn or a 30+ Wizard in Dungeons and Dragons, but who would be unwise to brag about such things to those who have no appreciation or understanding of them.

Two things suggest themselves here. First, know your audience. Know who will appreciate such accomplishments and who will, out of their own lack of consideration or hunger to be *greater than* in this world of nearly incessant one-up-manship, scorn them. Second, a little modesty goes a long way. Even if you are a grand high wizard, revealing this, in most cases, is of little value. Actions, as they say, speak louder than words. Even if you have accomplished or experienced amazing things, it is not always wise to reveal those things to everyone. There is a reason that the higher levels of esoteric development often involve vows of secrecy. It is not merely to keep powers from those who might abuse them. It is also to preserve the dignity of those who have them and to protect such societies from those who would ignorantly deride their value, evoking negative thinking in realms where thoughts are things and can have tremendous power. This is also the reason it is unwise to pursue one's infatuations and feelings of love when one's attentions have been rejected; one is demeaned by further pursuit unless this proceeds from a place of inner confidence and the principles of enchantment advise that we ever act from a calm and dignified center. Being seen as "needy" is seldom to one's benefit.

So it is that we elves walk among normal folk often allowing them to presume we are like them, only, perhaps, dressing somewhat unusually to their minds. We live our myth but, except among our own folk and those who might be open to it, we don't speak much of our myth. We live in our own worlds, and theirs, at the same time. They, in their narrowness, see only one world; we, in our openness, see myriad parallel dimensions.

This is true of many folks who work in the corporate world during the week and then live the "vampire" or other lifestyle on the weekends, dressing for each role as needed and essentially keeping these two worlds separate for fear of getting fired if they revealed their true nature, their personal myth. This need to keep the worlds separate, while unfortunately necessary, is often wise.

Past Life Experiences

Many people support their personal myth with tales of past life memories, claiming their were Napoleon, or Cleopatra, or this or that king, queen, notable, or by creating an elaborate story of how they came to be in hiding in this world. This is true of Otherkin and Elfin folk as well as many from the dominant culture. This is similar to some homeless person telling you that

183

he was once a millionaire. What can you say but: what happened? Or: that's too bad. Or: oh, really?

Whether these tales have substance or not in the linear world of consensual reality, they have real meaning in the non-linear world of the personal myth and of the psyché. Whether it is true that an individual was Napoleon in a past life is less important than the fact that this person resonates with the myth of Napoleon. It is quite possible, even likely, that an individual who thinks that she was Cleopatra in a past life, wasn't. However, this individual may have been someone similar, whose name and story has been lost in the annals of time and Cleopatra is the closest they can come to expressing this. And even if that is not true, it surely represents an aspiration for that individual. Such tales communicate to us what these individuals are striving to become via their personal myth. They are not usually a literal but rather a symbolic communication.

We might deride such individuals for the folly of creating a false past to make thems'elves seem more important or powerful than they are currently in this lifetime but, really, all they are telling us is that once they felt important, and probably loved and admired, and aspire toward this state again. For the elves the challenge is to give them, in as much as we can and in as much as it is good for their spirit, the support and encouragement for their myth that they need.

In some ways such individuals may seem somewhat pitiful (needy), but we should remember that those individuals who became exceptional individuals in the world, as Hillman (1997) tells us in the *Soul's Code*, often altered the story of their past. This is surely the case with Carlos Castaneda (Wallace, 2003) and in his books (1972) the sorcerer Don Juan often advised him to *erase this personal history* and become whoever he wished to be. Carlos surely did that. Changing one's life story to support one's personal myth is a common phenomena, most people do this by simply remembering their past differently or in a more favorable light and this is to be expected, even in some ways encouraged. This is also a method of freeing ones'elf from the limitations and expectations of others who would categorize one according to one's past. Elves and other magical and spiritual people often acquire new names to signify this new s'elf.

What is important in the personal myth, however, is not who you were, although many in the normal world might be swayed if you have a good enough story and enough charm, but who you are. Nearly all of us, if we manage to survive to old age, will be able to say, I was once young and strong. But the question remains, who are you now, and what is the power of your personality? It is not our personal history that matters so much in the long run, but the living vibration of our spirit; how that history and experience has transformed us.

The Curious Case of Carlos Castaneda

Richard De Mille (1976) in his books *Castaneda's Journey: The Power and the Allegory* and *The Don Juan Papers: Further Castaneda Controversies* (1980) with the help of experts in various academic fields studied Carlos Castaneda's works quite closely and concluded that his research, while Valid, was not Authentic. In other words, he and the others assisting him inferred that while Castaneda's books represented legitimate research that it was not carried on, for the most part, in the *field*, or in the deserts of Mexico, but rather in the UCLA library.

Most people, upon hearing this would decide that Castaneda was therefore a fake and not a real sorcerer at all. But it is the view of these elves that Castaneda's sorcery, magic and enchantment had almost nothing to do with being tutored by a sorcerer in the world of consensual reality, and everything to do with having a mentor/benefactor in the imaginal realms of being. The fact that he not only transformed his own life profoundly (Wallace, 2003) and created a very successful and viable personal myth but also created a series of enchanting books that captured the imagination of millions of individuals tends to validate this premise. Castaneda was a very real sorcerer/enchanter; he just didn't learn his sorcery in the Mexico of the material world, but the Mexico of the imaginal shamanic world.

One might ask, then why didn't he tell us that, as Zardoa indicated his imaginal explorations in this book; and the reason is clearly that in a world in which the material view of everything tends to predominate, imaginal explorations are, for the most part, discounted and denigrated. In academic circles, as we've seen earlier, they are often referred to as being *airy-fairy*. Yet, in reading Castaneda's books one can but wonder, is this real? Is this even possible? His books, by their very nature, speak of the imaginal and perceptual nature of reality. What he does, and does very well, is arouse our wonder and evoke the Mystery.

Drugs Vs. Imagination

This denigration of imaginal experiences is partially why so many folks seek the mystery in psychotropic drug experiences. Although, this is not completely so, for ancient shamans, who did not live in such materially oriented cultures, also used various plant and tree allies to aid them in their quest to communicate with the Otherworlds.

Many people also denigrate drug experiences. They view these experiences with the same disregard that they view dreams and designate them as hallucinations. Still drug experiences tend to be seen by those who do value them as having more validity than pure imaginal work and the reason is that while Active

Imagination and other imaginal practices have the conscious mind in control of the process of communicating with the normally unconscious realms of the psyché, psychédelics can plunge one directly into that Perilous Realm where the deep psyché takes charge. It seizes one and escorts one out of one's normal perceptions and takes one in a great rush into the nether worlds. It is not the conscious individual but the ally or the enemy within who takes charge.

This is the same reason, really, that the I Ching is often regarded as a more effective and potent oracle than the Tarot. The Tarot, having little exact textual definition, is very open to the interpretation of the individual reader, as well as, in our experience, the individual for whom it is being read. One often tends to interpret the result according to what one expects or wants to hear. The I Ching, however, while still needing some interpretation, has some very definite textual responses that can knock one for a loop and one gets the impression that one is definitely receiving the point of view of the spirits and not as much the bias of the reader.

All this is to say that in striving to live our personal myth, we also want it to be real. We want real experiences, valid magical experiences, which, alas, for those of us raised in a materialistic culture, is difficult to come by simply through imaginal explorations. This is not to say that imaginal experiences don't have validity, or that drug experiences aren't valid, but that these are best when reinforced by experiences in the material world, as we tried to demonstrate in this book, where we integrated the imaginal world, the dream world and normal experiences and interpreted them through the perceptual lens of the personal myth. It is not enough to draw an oracle, one must see if experience validates its prophecy. That is the scientific part of magic.

The Power of Fantasy

But lest we toss away the imaginal completely, let us remember that the imaginal realms have had profound effect upon the world. When an individual says that Jesus saved me or my life has been transformed through my religious practice, that individual is essentially saying that he/she has had a numinous imaginal psychological spiritual experience.

In fact, Christianity, Islam, Buddhism and every other religion, including Communism, that have profoundly transformed the world or an individual's life, are all systems of ideas that individuals experience in imaginal ways. Whether you believe Jesus suffered and died on the cross in consensual reality or not, the fact is all people who believe this are connecting to this idea "imaginally". Indeed, almost everything we believe about history is basically imaginal experience. If the victors write history, as we are often told and which seems to have great truth to it, then most history books are not far removed from historical fiction.

The simple fact is that due to our limited experience and understanding of the Universe, and due to our prejudices and our preconceptions, almost all that we understand about life is really based upon imaginal views of Life. If you've ever been misunderstood, and we expect you have, by someone who interpreted what you said or did not according to what you actually did or intended but according to their own preconceived expectations of your behavior, you will know how profoundly people live in their imaginal expectations.

Most elves simply accept this fact, and while we strive to discover the true nature of the world, we also understand the power of imagination, the power of fantasy. We learn our magic from various tomes of the esoteric arts, but we also find ours'elves, our magic and our culture inspired by novels. Obviously, the *Lord of the Rings* figures greatly into the works that inspire us, but there are others as well.

188

Some people, usually early on, base their personal myth on fantasy or fictional characters. They see thems'elves as being Legolas, or Aragorn or Gimli, etc. Like those who associate their character with Napoleon or Cleopatra, it is important to understand that these are indications of the direction of the individual's personal myth. But in the long run, it is important that the personal myth be unique. Every spirit seeks to become hir (his/her) own true s'elf, a s'elf which may be like Legolas but is not, in fact, a fictional character. That is the whole point; we are not trying to fictionalize ours'elves but to become more real, more authentic.

These elves once knew a young woman who was very excited by a friend of hers who claimed he was "one of the twelve". The "twelve" as it turned out was something from a legend used by Donovan on his song *Atlantis*. Once again, what this person was really saying was, I'm important. I'm a person of significance, a person of power. This individual had clearly been inspired by and related strongly to that particular myth.

These elves also integrate the magics that inspire us from novels into our own magic workings. In Nnedi Okorafor's novel *Akata Witch* (2011) a young girl learns her magic in Nigeria. Every time she learns a new magic, or develops a new magical/psychic skill, metal disks appear, as though falling from the sky, to signify this progress, the most potent of these being copper disks. Since these elves, like many other sorcerers love finding money and will always pick up a penny if we come across one (Wallace, 2003), we thought: what an interesting imaginal process to consider that every time we find money it is an indication of magical progress and this being particularly so when we find pennies (it makes the finding of pennies much more exciting).

But more than that we had some bracelets for years, one of them is made of copper, silver and bronze wire wound together that was specifically made for Zardoa and given to him as a birthday present over twenty years ago, another of copper, and a third made of tin with decorative filigree and red and blue stones from India. He almost never wore these bracelets that are also, in a sense, metal disks. So he began wearing them as a symbol of his aspiration to magical progress. He incorporated the imaginal, the fantasy into his living reality. In that way, he took the elements of fantasy and made them real.

In another example, Laini Taylor's novel *Daughter of Smoke and Bone* (2012) speaks of beads that are given and serve as talismans and magical powers. When one makes a wish upon the bead the wish comes true and the bead turns to dust. A few days after reading this, we were walking down the street to the local grocery store and we found a bracelet that had numerous and various beads and charms on it, including a charm of a rose, a heart and one with a rhinestone in it, as well as assorted black, white and filigreed copper colored beads. We have not as yet, made any wishes on these beads, but we thought, what an interesting sign that we should find this bracelet while reading that book, a bit of a magical synchronicity. Now, we expect that if we did make a wish on a bead, it probably wouldn't turn to dust instantly any more than the wish is likely to come true immediately, but still, there are wishes there waiting to be made and we know if we did make them they would eventually come true, just as the beads will eventually and inevitably turn to dust. In the meantime, we keep them in our magic, increasing and storing up their energy.

Our point is that fantasy, and the imaginal, can be inspiring and what is inspiring *is* magical and can be easily and successfully integrated into one's personal myth in a realistic fashion. The imaginal realm, while those who pretend to be scientifically minded often discount it, has had and continues to have profound effects upon the world and we can utilize that power to transform our own lives through our personal myth. Embrace the things that inspire you.

Every One Is the Hero of Hir Own Myth

Remember, everyone is the hero of hir own myth. This is true even in those individuals who actively support another's myth, as in those individuals, such as parents who sacrifice for their children. In these instances, the hero is the one who makes the sacrifice. John Milton in his poem *On His Blindness* wrote, "They also serve who only stand and wait." We each have our place or role and if we fulfill it properly, the best that we can, we are heroes.

Despite novels, movies and television shows that continually speak of *the One*, it is important to remember that everyone is meant to be the hero, to fulfill hirs'elf perfectly, to find hir true place as a star in the Universe (Crowley, 1976). There *is* only *One*, as the Highlander movies tell us, only One Unique You.

This aspect of the One, the most Powerful heroic figure, was dealt with quite tongue-in-cheek in the Buffy series, where there was the *One Slayer*, but also other Slayers. Elven myths thus (see appendix) tend to be about a group, as in the *Lord of the Rings* and the *Hobbit*, and yes, *Buffy*, of heroic figures with various talents and abilities joining together on the great quest.

But this brings us to the question: do heroes need villains? We expect that the orcs and goblins in the *Lord of the Rings* had they really existed would have thought themselves heroic figures also and surely the Nazis conceived of themselves as being heroic. Few people consciously strive to be villains or to be evil, and even then, these individuals tend to see this as a heroic act of Mastery and Power, a triumph of Will and Spirit.

By accepting that everyone is a hero, or really aspires to be, each in hir own way and is meant to be heroic, we put aside our ego and diminish our self importance, as spiritual practices advise us to do, while retaining our personal sense of confident s'elfhood. Being the hero isn't about being better than others, it is about being the best one can be.

In the long run, these conflicts between villains and heroes are mere inconveniences upon the way. The true Quest is the quest for knowledge and understanding in the material world, the scientific quest; the quest for spiritual understanding, the mystical quest; the quest for inner understanding, the psychological quest; the quest to find one's true kin, the romantic, loving family quest that when extended to the Universal plane becomes the soulful quest; and the quest to become the immortal powerful being you are destined to become, the quest of the true s'elf, the quest of spirit to transform the personal myth into reality.

Some people may wonder why

if we could live in Faerie,

would we bother to live in this world.

But we elves see

Faerie being born all around us.

BIBLIOGRAPHY:

Adler, M. (1979). Drawing down the moon: witches, druids, goddess-worshippers, and other pagans in america today. Boston, Ma.: Beacon Press.

Anderson, R. (1998). Celtic oracles: a new system for spiritual growth and divination. N.Y., N.Y.: Harmony Books.

Arlisson, R. (2005). The witching way of the hollow hill: The gramarye of the folk who dwell below the mound. Los Angeles, Ca.: Pendraig Publishing.

Arnold. M. A.; Windling, T. (eds.) (1986). Borderland. N. Y., N. Y.: Roc.

Avens, R. (1982). Imaginal body: Para-jungian reflections on soul, imagination and death. Washington, D. C.: University Press of America.

Aziz, R. (1990). C.G. Jung's psychology of religion and synchronicity. Albany, NY: State University of New York Press.

Bailey, A. (1971). Esoteric astrology. N. Y., N. Y.: Lucis Publishing Company.

Bardon, F. (1975). The practice of magical evocation: Instructions for invoking spirits from the spheres surrounding us. Wuppertal, Germany: Dieter Ruggeberg.

Baudino, G. (1989). Strands of starlight. N. Y., N. Y.: New American Library

Blavatsky, H. P. (1974). The secret doctrine. Los Angeles, Ca.: Theosophy Company.

Blavatsky, H. P. (2004). Occultism of the secret doctrine. Whitefish, Montana.: Kessinger Publications, LLC.

Bolen, J. S. (1984). Goddesses in everywoman. New York, N.Y.: Harper and Row.

Bond, D. S. (1993). Living myth. Boston: Shamballa Publications, Inc..

Bosnak, R. (1988). A little course in dreams. Boston, Ma.: Shamballa Publications, Inc..

Briggs, K. (1967). The fairies: In tradition and literature. London, U.K.: Routledge and Kegan Paul, Ltd..

Briggs, K. (1978). The vanishing people: Fairy lore and legends. N.Y., N. Y.: Pantheon Books.

Briggs, K. (1979). Abbey lubbers, banshees and boggarts: An illustrated encyclopedia of fairies. N.Y., N. Y.: Pantheon Books.

Butler, W. E. (1959). The magician: His training and work. London, U. K.: The Aquarian Press.

Campbell, J. (1949). The hero with a thousand faces. Princeton, N.J., Princeton University Press.

Campbell, J. (1968). Masks of god: Creative mythology. New York: Viking.

Campbell, J. (2000). Historical development of mythmaking. myth and mythmaking. (Henry A. Murray, ed.). Boston, Ma.: Beacon Press.

Carding, E. (2012). Faery craft: Weaving connections with the enchanted realm. Woodbury, MN.: Llewellyn Publications.

Carr-Gomm,P., Carr-Gomm, S. (1994). The druid animal oracle: Working with the sacred animals of the druid tradition. N.Y., N.Y.: Fireside, Simon and Schuster.

Castaneda, Carlos. (1972) Journey to ixtlan. New York, New York.: Simon & Schuster.

Castaneda, C. (2000). The active side of infinity. New York, N.Y.: Perennial.

Charters, D. (author) Pilarski, M. (ed.) Forty years with the fairies. Arcata, Ca.: R. J. Stewart Books.

Cherryh, C. J. (1997). The dreaming tree. N. Y., N. Y.: DAW.

Chopra, Deepak (1995) The way of the wizard: Twenty spiritual lessons for creating the world that you want, N.Y., N.Y.:Harmony Books, Crown Publishers, Inc.

Conger, J. P. (1988). Jung and reich: The body as shadow. Berkeley, CA: North Atlantic Books.

Corbett, L. (1996). The religious function of the psyché. N.Y., N.Y.: Routledge.

Crowley, A. (1976). Magick: In theory and practice. N.Y.,N.Y.: Dover Publications.

Daniels, K. N., Daniels, V. (2003). Tarot d'amour: Find love, sex, and romance in the cards. York Beach, Me.: Red Wheel/Weiser, LLC.

De Mille, R. (1976). Castaneda's journey: The power and the allegory. Santa Barbara, Ca.: Capra.

De Mille, R. (1980). The don juan papers: Further castaneda controversies. Santa Barbara, Ca.: Ross-Erickson.

Deren, M. (1953). Divine horsemen: The living gods of haiti. New Paltz, N.Y.: McPherson and Company.

De Vere, N. (2004) The dragon legacy: The secret history of an ancient bloodline. San Diego, Ca.: The Book Tree.

Domino, G. (Oct. 1976). Compensatory aspects of dreams: An empirical test of jung's theory. Journal of Personality and Social Psychology, Vol 34(4), 658-662.

Douglas, N., Slinger, P. (1979). The secret dakini oracle. Rochester, Vt.: Destiny Books.

Eagle Feather, K. (1995). A toltec path. Charlottesville, Va.: Hampton Roads Publishing Company, Inc.

Evans-Wentz, W.Y. (1966). Fairy-Faith in celtic countries. New Hyde Park, N.Y.: University Books, Inc..

Fadiman, J., Frager, R. (1974). Personality and personal growth. Upper Saddle River, N.J.: Pearson Education, Inc..

Feinstein, D.; Granger, D. ;Krippner, S., (1988) Mythmaking and human development., Journal of Humanistic Psychology; 28 (3), p23, 28.

Feinstein, D.; Krippner, S. (1997) The mythic path: Discovering the guiding stories of your past -- Creating a vision for your future. New York, N.Y.: A Jeremy P. Tarcher/ Putnam Book.

Feinstein, D.;Krippner, S.; Mortifee, A., (1998) New myths for a new millennium. Futurist, 32 (2).

Feinstein, D. (1998), At play in the fields of the mind: Personal myths as fields of information. Journal of Humanistic Psychology, 38(3), 71-109.

Frazer, J. G. (1951). The golden bough: A study in magic and religion. N.Y., N.Y.: MacMillan Company. Originally published in 1922.

Gardner, L. (2003). Realm of the ring lords: The myth and magic of the grail quest. Gloucester, Ma.: Fair Winds Press.

Gendlin, E. T. (1986). Let your body interpret your dreams. Wilmette, Il.: Chiron Publications.

Gomes, M. E., Kanner, A. D., Roszak, T. (Ed.)(1995). Ecopsychology: Restoring the earth, healing the mind. San Francisco, Ca.: Sierra Club Books.

Graves, R. (1966). The white goddess: A historical grammar of poetic myth. N.Y., N.Y.: Farrar, Straus and Giroux. Originally published in 1948.

Gray, M. (1992). The gateway of liberation and spiritual laws: Rules of the evolutionary arc. Tahlequah, Oklahoma.: Sparrow Hark Press.

Green, C. E., Lenihan, E. (2004). Meeting the other crowd: The fairy stories of hidden Ireland. New York, N. Y. Tarcher.

Grimm, W. C. (1957). The book of trees. Harrisburg, Pa.: The Stackpole Company.

Hamaker-Zondag, K. (1997). Tarot as a way of life. York Beach, Me.: Samuel Weiser, Inc.

Hannah, Barbara. (2001). Encounters with the soul: Active imagination. Wilmette, Il. Chiron Publications.

Harner, M. (1982). The way of the shaman. New York: Harper and Row.

Hillman, J. (1997). The soul's code: In search of character and calling. New York: Warner Books, Inc.

Hopcke, R. H. (1997). There are no accidents: Synchronicity and the stories of our lives. N.Y., N.Y.: Riverhead Books.

Houston, J. (1996). A mythic life: Learning to live our greater story. San Francisco, Ca. : Harper.

Ipcar, D. (1973). The queen of spells. N.Y., N.Y.: Viking Press.

James, J.: Weeks, D. (1996). Eccentrics: A study of sanity and strangeness. New York, N.Y.: Kodansha International.

Johnson, R. A. (1986). Inner work. New York: HarperCollins.

Jung, C. G. (1956). Symbols of transformation, Collected works of C. G. Jung. 5. Princeton, N. J.: Princeton University Press.

Jung, E. (1957). Animus and anima. N.Y., N.Y.: Spring Publications. Originally published in 1934.

Jung, C. G. (1959a). Aion: Researches into the phenomenology of the self. New York. Bollingen Foundation, Inc.

Jung, C. G. (1959b). Psychological types. In V. Laszlo (Ed.), The basic writings of C. G. Jung. (R. F. Hull, Trans.). New York: Random House. (Original work published 1938).

Jung, C. G. (1959c). The relations between the ego and unconscious. In V. Laszlo (Ed.), The basic writings of C. G. Jung. (R. F. Hull, Trans.). New York: Random House. (Original work published 1938).

Jung, C. G. (1960a).(R.F.C. Hull, Trans.). Synchronicity: An acausal connecting principle. N.Y., N.Y.: Princetown University Press.

Jung, C. G. (1960b). A review of the complex theory. (R.F.C. Hull, Trans.). In H. Read, M. Fordham, & G. Adler (Eds.), Collected works of C. G. Jung (Vol 8, pp.92-104). New York, NY: Pantheon Books, Inc.. (Original work published in 1946)

Jung, C. G. (1962) (commentary). The secret of the golden flower. Wilhelm, R. (trans.) New York: Harcourt Brace and Co.

Jung, C. G. (1971). The portable Jung. (Campbell, J. ed.). New York, Viking Penguin, Inc..

Jung, C. G. (1983). The essential Jung. New York. MJF Books.

Jung, C. G. (1989). Memories, dreams and reflections. (Jaffe, A. ed.). New York: Vintage Books.

Karcher, S. (1997). How to use the I ching. London, U.K.: Element.

Keightley, T. (1978). The world guide to gnomes, fairies, elves and other little people. N.Y., N.Y.: Avenel Books. Originally published in 1880 as The Fairy Mythology.

Kelly, G.A. (1963). A theory of personality N. Y., N. Y.: W.W. Norton.

Larsen, S. (1988). The shaman's doorway: Opening imagination to power and myth. Barrytown, N.Y.: Station Hill Press.

Larrington, C. (Trans.) (1999). The poetic edda. Oxford, G. B.: Oxford World's Classics.

Larsen, S. (1996). The mythic imagination: The quest for meaning through personal mythology. Rochester, Vt.: Inner Traditions International.

Larson, C. (2013). Quantum jumps: An extraordinary science of happiness and prosperity. Berkeley, Ca.: Reality Shifters.

Leary, T. (1982). Changing my mind, among others. N. J.: Prentice Hall.

Leary, T. (1995). High priest. Berkeley, Ca.: Ronin Publishing.

Lord Dunsany. (1999). The king of elfland's daughter. N. Y., N. Y.: Del Rey.

Love, M. C., Sterling, R. W. (2011). What's behind your belly button? A psychological perspective of the intelligence of human nature and gut instinct. Charleston, S. C.: CreateSpace.

Lupa. (2007). A field guide to otherkin. Stafford, UK.: Megalithica Books of Immanion Press.

MacManus, S. (1944). The story of the irish race: A popular history of ireland. N.Y., N.Y.: Devin-Adair Company.

Mahrer, A. R. (2001). What can the clinician trust— research? theory? clinical knowledge?. American Journal of Psychotherarpy, 55 (3).

Matthews, J. (1995). The celtic shaman's pack. London, U.K.: Elemental Books, Ltd.

May, R. (1988). Paulus: Tillich as a spiritual teacher. Dallas, Tx.: Saybrook Publishing Company, Inc.

McAdams, D. P. (1983). The stories we live by: Personal myths and the making of the self. New York: Guilford Press.

Metraux, A. (1972). Voodoo in haiti. H. Charteris, (trans.). N.Y., N.Y.: Schocken Books, Inc. Originally published in 1959.

Mindell, A. (1993). The shaman's body: A new shamanism for transforming health, relationships, and community. San Francisco, Ca.: Harper San Francisco.

Mindell, A. (2001). The dreammaker's apprentice. Charlottesville, Va.: Hamption Roads Publishing Co. Inc.

Murray, C., Murray, L. (1988). The celtic tree oracle: A system of divination. N.Y., N.Y.: St. Martin's Press.

Narby, J. (1998). The cosmic serpent: DNA and the origins of knowledge. N.Y., N.Y.: Jeremy P. Tarcher/Putnam.

Okorafor, N. (2011). Akata witch. New York, New York.: Viking Juvenile.

Piaget, J. (1950). The psychology of intelligence. New York, N.Y.: International Universities Press.

Powell, A. E. (1927). The astral body: and other astral phenomena. Wheaton, Il.: Quest Books.

Raff, J. (1997a). The felt vision. In D. F. Sandner & S. H. Wong, (Eds.). The sacred heritage: The influence of shamanism on analytical psychology. (pp. 79 - 90). N.Y., N.Y.: Routledge.

Raff, J. (1997b). The ally. In D. F. Sandner & S. H. Wong, (Eds.). The sacred heritage: The influence of shamanism on analytical psychology. (pp. 111-121). N.Y., N.Y.: Routledge.

Raff, J. (2000). Jung and the alchemical imagination. Berwick, Me.: Nicolas-Hays, Inc.

Ratti, O., Westbrook, A. (1973). Secrets of the samurai: The martial arts of feudal japan. Rutland, Vt.: Charles E. Tuttle Company.

Reifler, S. (1974). I ching. N. Y., N. Y.: Bantam Books.

Regardie, I. (1972). The tree of life: A study in magic. York Beach, Me.: Samuel Weiser, Inc.

Rogers, C. (1961). On becoming a person. Boston, Ma.: Houghton Mifflin Company.

Roth, J. E. (1997). American elves: An encyclopedia of little people from the lore of 380 ethnic groups of the western hemisphere. Jefferson, N.C.: McFarland.

Rudhyar, D. (1973). An astrological mandala: The cycle of transformations and its 360 symbolic phases. N.Y., N.Y.: Random House.

Ryan, R. E. (2002). Shamanism and the psychology of c. g. jung: The great circle. London, G. B.: Vega.

Sheldrake, R. (1995). The Presence of the past: Morphic resonance & the habits of nature. Rochester, Vt.: Inner Traditions International.

Silver Elves (2001a). The book of elven runes. Sebastopol, Ca.: Silver Elves Publications.

Silver Elves (2001b). The magical elven love letters, vol. 1. Sebastopol, Ca.: Silver Elves Publications.

Silver Elves (2011a). Eldafaryn: True tales of magic from the lives of the silver elves. Charleston, S. C.: CreateSpace.

Silver Elves (2007, 2011b). The magical elven love letters, vol. 2. Charleston, S. C.: CreateSpace.

Silver Elves (2012a). The elven book of changes: A magical interpretation of the I Ching. Charleston, S. C.: CreateSpace.

Silver Elves (2012b). The elven book of dreams: A magical oracle of faerie. Charleston, S. C.: CreateSpace.

Silver Elves (2012c). The magical elven love letters, vol. 3. Charleston, S. C.: CreateSpace.

Silver Elves (2012d). Through the mists of faerie: A magical guide to the wisdom teachings of the ancient elven. Charleston, S. C.: CreateSpace.

Silver Elves (2012e) vol. 1. The book of elven magick: The philosophy and enchantments of the seelie elves. Charleston, S. C.: CreateSpace.

Silver Elves (2012f) vol. 2. The book of elven magick: The philosophy and enchantments of the seelie elves. Charleston, S. C.: CreateSpace.

Silver Elves (2012g) Arvyndase (Silverspeech): A short course in the magical language of the silver elves. Charleston, S. C.: CreateSpace.

Silver Elves (2013a). The elven way: The magical path of the shining ones. Charleston, S. C.: CreateSpace.

Silver Elves (2013b). Liber ælph: Words of guidance from the silver elves to our magical children. Charleston, S. C.: CreateSpace.

Silver Elves (2014a) vol. 1. The elf magic mail: Book 1 the original letters of the elf queen's daughters with commentary by the silver elves. Charleston, S. C.: CreateSpace.

Silver Elves (2014b) vol. 2. The elf magic mail: Book 2 the original letters of the elf queen's daughters with commentary by the silver elves. Charleston, S. C.: CreateSpace.

Some, M.P. (1998). The healing wisdom of africa: Finding life purpose through nature, ritual, and community. N.Y., N.Y.: Jeremy P. Tarcher/Putnam.

Soukhanov, A. H. (ed.) (1984). Webster's II new riverside university dictionary. Boston, Ma.: Houghton Mifflin, Company.

Starhawk (1982). Dreaming the dark: Magic, sex and politics. Boston, Ma.: Beacon Press.

Starhawk (1989). The spiral dance: A rebirth of the ancient religion of the great goddess. N.Y., N.Y.: Harper and Row. First published in 1979.

Stein, M. (1998). Jung's map of the soul. Chicago, Il.: Open Court.

Suino, N. (1994). The art of japanese swordmanship: A manual of eishin-ryu iaido. N.Y., N.Y.: Weatherhill, Inc..

Taylor, J. (1983). Dream work: Techniques for discovering the creative power in dreams. Mawah, N.J.: Paulist Press.

Taylor, L. (2012). Daughter of smoke and bone. New York, New York.: Little, Brown Books for Young Readers.

Tolkien, J.R.R. (1977a). On fairy-stories. In tree and leaf. London: George Allen and Unwin, Ltd..

Tolkien, J.R.R. (1977b) Silmarillion. Boston, Ma.: Houghton Mifflin Company.

Von Franz, M. L. (1977). Individuation in fairytales. Dallas, Tx.: Spring Publications, Inc.

Von Franz, M. L. (1980). On divination and synchronicity: The psychology of meaningful chance. Toronto, Canada.: Inner City Books.

Waite, A. E. (1974). The quest of the golden stairs: A mystery of kinghood in faerie. Hollywood, Ca.: Newcastle Publishing Company.

Wallace, A. (2003). Sorcerer's apprentice: My life with carlos castaneda. Berkeley, Ca.: Frog, Ltd.

Warrington, Freda. (2010). Elfland. N. Y., N. Y.: Tor Fantasy.

Wicker, C. (2005). Not in kansas anymore: A curious tale of how magic is transforming America. San Francisco, Ca.: Harper.

Wilber, K. (1981). No boundary: Eastern and western approaches to personal growth. Boulder, Co.: Shambala Publications, Inc.

Wilhelm, H., Baynes, C. (trans.). (1967). I ching. Princeton, N.J.: Princeton University Press.

Williamson, M. (1997). The healing of america. N.Y., N.Y.: Simon and Schuster.

Yu, A. C. (trans. and ed.). (1977). The journey to the west, vol. 1. Chicago, Il.: University of Chicago Press.

As Above, So Below,

As Within, So Without,

What goes around, Comes Around,

And we elves sit in the center

And watch with fascination.

APPENDIX:

The Return of Faerie:
An Emerging Mythology

"I HAVE LONGED FOR THY WAYS IN THE MORNING AND I HAVE FOUND THEE IN THE EVENING STAR: YESTERDAY, TODAY AND FOREVER IS WRITTEN ON ALL THY GATES."
(WAITE, 1974, P. 164)

The New Mythos and the Age of Aquarius

As one of the prerequisites to entering the Depth Psychology program, these elves had to take a course entitled *Myths, Dreams and Symbols.* In our very first class our instructor, Mary Gomes, the eco psychologist, had us watch a video in which Joseph Campbell the mythologist was asked about a new myth emerging to replace the dying myths of our time and he replied that he saw no sign of one doing so. We thought this over through the evening and came to the conclusion that, at least from our point of view, he was incorrect. We can understand why he didn't recognize the new myth, since he is used to examining existing myths rather than emerging ones. But, we think also, he most likely dismissed the emerging myth as a fad rather than as being the genuine birth of a new mythos.

The new myth of which we speak centers on the idea of the Age of Aquarius. It can be distinguished from older myths by several factors that each in its way relates to the difference between the Age of Pisces and the Aquarian Age. The theme of the Piscean Age is dichotomous. It functions in a Good vs. Bad, either/or, right vs. wrong, you're either with us or against us, mode. The symbol for Pisces resembles inverted parentheses with a single line connecting them at their center. The symbol for Aquarius, on the other hand, is two waves moving in the same direction but at different frequencies. Instead of right and wrong, we have a multiplicity of equally valid realities/lifestyles. George Kelly's Personal Construct psychology (Fadiman, 1974) is a prime example of Aquarian thought as it confronts and seeks to transform dichotomous Piscean attitudes.

While the Piscean Age functioned primarily on zero sum games (there can only be one winner ~ look at the Highland series myth) the Aquarian mythos is developing Non-Competitive and Cooperative Games. A typical motto of the Aquarian principle is the *win-win* situation. While the Piscean mind insists on an either/or point of view, a current Aquarian buzz world is *inclusiveness*. While Pisceans think of resources as a pie with just so many slices that everyone fights over, winner takes all or what's left after the fighting, the Aquarian speaks of sustainability and of renewable resources. In occult circles, there are seven rays of manifestation (Blavatsky, 2004). The motto of the fourth ray through the Piscean Age has been "Harmony through Conflict" (Bailey, 1971, pp. 327-328). This point of view is easily seen in our court system in which two opposing forces battle under the theory that the truth will emerge through their conflict. The motto of the fourth ray for the Aquarian Age, however, is "Harmony through Diversity" and you will see bumper stickers proclaiming this new credo as they encourage us to "Celebrate Diversity."

The Piscean Mythos ever centers on a hero and often his less than adequate sidekick, who overcomes great evil and saves the world. The Aquarian Mythos nearly always is centered on a group of heroes, sometimes all inadequate by thems'elves, who band to together to accomplish the great Quest, whatever it might be. The *Lord of the Rings* is a wonderful example of an emerging Aquarian Myth. What makes it important and is vital to the Aquarian Myth, is that it is not merely a group that overcomes the forces of Darkness, but a group of diverse individuals each adding their particular talent, skill and idiosyncrasy to the united effort. The character Boromir, however, is an exception to this. He is an example of someone who is unable to fully embrace the Aquarian mode, seeking rather to be the One, the savior of humanity, and thus he is seduced by the Ring, the example of Piscean domination. Galadriel on the other hand, knew that in taking the ring she would be sucked into that role of dominator, and choose to give up power rather than fall into that trap.

In real life terms, the founding of the United States was a bold experiment and step into the Aquarian Age. And while the idea of evil is central to Piscean thought: "There is no good without bad"; it is not necessary in the Aquarian mode. It can be there, but in Aquarian thought, good is not necessarily juxtaposed to evil, but rather to better and best. For the Aquarian, life is not about overcoming evil and being right against what is wrong, but rather being the best one can be and constantly improving ones'elf and one's situation. Aquarians function on a "live and let live" attitude. For the Piscean, there is only one true religion. For the Aquarian, the only right path is the path that is right for you.

The fact that this mythos is emerging at this time is no mere accident. It is, as its name implies, a progression of Zodiacal influence and thus was prophesied ages ago. Just as we can look forward two thousand years and know the Aquarian Mythos will eventually and inevitably give way to the Golden Age of Capricorn. The Aquarian Mythos is the key to overcoming the myriad problems that we now face in the world due to intransigent Piscean thought forms. Aquarian thought is literally the salvation of the world.

One might ask, however, how Aquarian thought is all that different from the Piscean. After all, as in the *Lord of the Rings*, it is still a tale of good vs. evil. However, Piscean thought demands domination. There is only one side/form seen as good. The Aquarian mode, like democracy, seeks to ensure freedom. Evil is thus defined as that which would take away or overly limit that freedom. Aquarian thought is thus seen not in opposition to Piscean thought, again good vs. evil, but as a step further. It is an evolution of that thought. The good has diversified. It is no longer Black vs. White, but a rainbow of colors, which incorporate black and white, but stand against a narrowing of the color range.

The Mythologized Past

These elves have always felt alienated from most of modern society. Even though we were raised using English, We've always felt that English was a foreign language to us. Over the past twenty-five years, we've heard from thousands of people from all over the world who feel the same way (see our book Arvyndase (Silverspeech): a short course in the magical language of the Silver Elves (2012g)). Like most Americans, we can trace our ancestry to other continents. Both of us, Silver Flame and Zardoa, however, include Scottish in our ancestry. We've long wondered, what were our Scottish ancestors before they were Scottish. The Scots (who were Irish Celts, since Ireland used to be called Scoti by the Romans, (MacManus, 1973)) migrated to Scotland around 3 C. E. Before that, for at least a thousand years or more, Scotland or Alba, was inhabited by the Picts or Pict-Sidhe. Evans-Wentz tells us in his book *the Faery Faith in the Celtic Countries* of a Cornish form of elf called a Piskey (mentioned previously in the book. Actually, I have a postcard from Cornwall with a Piskey featured on the cover.) He traces the derivation of that word and says that in Devon the word piskey would be pronounced pixie. He goes on to demonstrate that the word that is piskey in one dialect and pixie in another comes out as Picty in yet another. Thus he surmises that the ancient Picts, our ancestors, are the same folk that some call piskey and others pixie. Thus these elves ancient Scottish ancestors were likely to have been the Sidhe (the faerie folk) from Ireland or the Picts, pixies of Alba.

If we continued in that vein with our other ancestors, we would tend to trace Zardoa's Welsh ancestors to the Piskeys/pixies, his French ancestors would be the Fae, Fe or Faery, his English ancestors would be the Brownies and his Dutch and Silver Flame's Germanic ancestors would be the Albs or Aelfs or Elves. Of course, we have no proof. The Picts were the last of a prehistoric folk who barely made it into historical tradition before they merged with their cousins the Scoti. We only have our feeling, our inner conviction that we are of a different race (race used in this case in the old sense such as the French race, German race or Japanese race), a different culture and people who, for the most part, have forgotten themselves.

It would be nice to think of our ancestors as the advanced and civilized folk of Tolkien's books and in a sense they were. But it is also helpful to understand that they were, in effect, European Aborigines. To understand their culture it helps to examine the cultures of Native Americans, for their situation was quite similar. The Picts were, in fact, such a fierce people that when the Romans invaded Britain they feared them so much that they built a stone wall (called Haridan's wall after the general who had it built) clear across the island to keep them from raiding south.

Of course, if we tell most folks that we are elves, they think that we're kidding, or perhaps crazy and so forth. Our people as an organized culture, for the most part, have been gone from this Earth for such a long time that most people simply have come to believe that we were a myth. Imagine the difference if we told people we were Native American. Imagine what life would be like for a Native American if their culture had been so far dissolved that no one even believed they had ever existed.

Interestingly, the mythologizing of our faerie people, easily seen in Tolkien as well as other works, can be observed with the Native Americans as well. They are in the process of becoming a Mythic People of great magical powers and spiritual propensities. If it were not for the fact that there are still Native Americans to whom one can compare the Myth, they would be Mythologized entirely.

Since for the most part, we are talking about prehistory, there is very little that we can provide as fact in regard to our Elfin heritage. This dilemma is not ours alone, but shared unknowingly by almost everyone. A simple look at the process of genetic progression will easily demonstrate this. We each had two parents, four grandparents in the 20th century. In the 19th century, we had eight great-grandparents, 16 great, great-grandparents, and 32 great, great, great. In the 18th century, we're talking about 64, 128, and 256. If we continued this process merely back to the year 1,000 C. E., we come up with a figure of 4, 294, 967, 296 possible genetic contributors to the DNA that composes us. Even eliminating the 294, 967, 296 to account for incest and inbreeding, that is a hefty sum. (Note that when DNA is taken for ancestry studies they are looking at your mother's, mother's, mother's mother and so on or your father's, father's father, which narrows it down a bit.) And it just gets larger as one goes backward, while the overall population in the past diminishes until we apparently come to one female (and we expect male) in Africa. From whom did we inherit our genes? It is, at least at this point, scientifically impossible to know precisely. Although we can determine the group we belong to that diverged from our African originators as they moved into Europe and began splitting up and going in different directions, if they did in fact leave Africa. Still, saying you are from this group or that tells us little when we know so little about those cultures. We elves, at least, are cast continually back upon our own instincts. We elven have a saying, "Ultimately, no one but an elf would be interested in being elven."

While it would be nice to be able to prove we are descended from elves, in the long run it doesn't really matter. The simple fact is, while elves may never have existed previously, except in Fairy Tales, We Do Now. While most people are dependent upon their ancestors as near as they can remember them, for the definition of their being, we elven are linked to our visions of the future. We are not what our ancestors were, but rather what our children and we, in future lifetimes, will be. Our claim to being elfin comes not so much from what others have done previously, but what we are doing now. It is an act of magic/enchantment. By living our lives as elves, we become, by manifestation, Elven.

When folks write to us as elves and we respond to them we almost always sign our letters, the Silver Elves ... very seldom do we sign them Silver Flame or Zardoa for the Silver Elves. This sometimes creates an incredible ambivalence in some folks, but we decided ages ago that our path was a path of service and was not about creating a charismatic leader figure (Piscean thinking), but about helping each elf to realize their own unique being (Aquarian/Elvish thought). We have dedicated ours'elves to that purpose and continue to do so.

Remember the story earlier in this book about someone calling Zardoa a Living Myth? Then fifteen years later, someone else did the same thing. Then about 15 years after that another person said something similar. Notice that in the first two instances, Zardoa was the Living Myth, a basic Piscean energy, the individual as the Mythos. However, in the third instance, it is we, as Silver Elves, who are referred to as Living Myths. And evolution has taken place, the Piscean heroic individual has evolved into the Aquarian group of individuals, the myth has become Elven.

Due to this, out in the world a Myth has been set free. It is the myth of the Living Elves. In the future, when people ask someone if elves ever existed they will be able to point to us and say, "Yes, they did," as well as, "Yes, we do!"

The Return of Faerie: The Prophecy

C. J. Cherryh, who most often writes Sci-Fi novels, also writes fantasy books including a number about the Sidhe (pronounced *she* (called Sith in Scotland)) the high elven of Irish/Scottish myth. In *the Dreaming Tree* (also known as *Ealdwood Stories* or *Arafel's Stories*), which is composed of two books, the *Dream Stone* and the *Tree of Swords and Jewels*, we follow the story of Arafel, the last elf on earth and her efforts to hold off the Dark Forces that would overtake mankind. In the end, two things bring about the victory of Arafel and that is a human who becomes elfin and the ancient elves returning to her side to battle the darkness. The result of this conflict is the Return of Faerie to the Earth, the merging of the realms. Note this merging of the realms is also the theme of Lord Dunsany's (1999) novel *the King of Elfland's Daughter*, one of the works that deeply influenced and inspired Tolkien.

In Gael Baudino's *Strands* series, Miriam, a human girl in Medieval Europe is transformed into an elf. She becomes, in time, the last of her kind until in modern times she finds and awakens other elfin among those who previously thought they were normal humans, although they always felt alienated from affectionless humanity.

The *Bordertown* series, beginning with *Borderland* (Arnold, 1986), is a group of books filled with short stories, as well as a few novels, by various authors taking place in the shared world of Bordertown. Bordertown exists somewhere in the near future when Elfland and the Normal World have merged in a city in

212

which magic and technology both work inconsistently and elves and humans also intermingle in an uneasy alliance and occasional hostility.

Elfland is a novel by Freda Warrington (2010) about elfin-like folk separated from their homeland by a closed portal endeavoring to reopen it to allow passage between the worlds. In it, one of the characters, by hanging out with the elven-like folk, becomes one hers'elf.

Tolkien (1977a, p. 28) wrote, "An essential power of Faerie is thus the power of making immediately effective by the will the visions of 'fantasy'." To most folks, these are just fantasy stories, but to the elfin, these are prophecies of the Return of Faerie. Of course, most think that Faerie is a place that exists apart from the Earth or is a parallel realm connected to the Earth to which they can escape. In a sense, this is so. Faerie does exist and occasionally under the influence of extreme circumstances or botanical intoxication one can go there for a time. But to stay there, to have it born upon the Earth, we must transform not the Earth so much as ours'elves. For it is not that the Elves will come to save the Earth and humanity, but that humanity must become more Elfin in order to save the Earth and thems'elves.

According to the Ancient Wisdom Traditions (Blavatsky, 1974), we are currently in the fifth sub-race of the fifth root race. This race is the most mental of all races but still very much driven by emotional impulses, which is to say they are in their heads mostly, but not necessarily logical. (Here we are distinguishing emotions from feeling. Feeling being a product of one's inner being, whereas emotions are a product of the mind. (Love, Sterling, 2011). We are approaching the time when the first fore-castes of the sixth sub-race will appear. These beings are still very mental, being of the fifth root race, but in a more direct, intuitive and feeling way. They will be thus more in touch with their unconscious and be more s'elf realized beings. They will be more attuned to what Jung defined as the Self. We

213

might get the idea from this that humankind is progressing as a whole and that there will be a progression from one sub-race to another in toto. But that is not the case. The sixth sub-race is the emergence of a distinct people and if our understanding of the Aquarian nature of the period is accurate, then it is really an emergence of numerous sub-species of humanity who hold one essential quality in common, a mutual tolerance for diversity.

The Starlight Path

The great Elfin sage, prophet, philosopher, psychiatrist, scientist and, yes, mythologist, Tymlyre (Leary, 1982) theorized that of the next 100 people we are likely to meet, each will, in time, evolve into a separate species. According to this theorist, the solution to all of humanity's problems is to be found in space. As we leave the planet and begin creating mini-earths in space we will also begin creating independent communities, communities of feminists, communities of vegetarians, communities of elves and so forth. Then, in truth, the Aquarian Age will have been initiated fully.

On her CD *Waterbearer* (Aquarius is the waterbearer and is related to Tarot major arcana 17, the Star), Sally Oldfield sings, "It's written on the walls of stone in starlight, there is a path across the night." Is it a coincidence that same CD has a tribute to Tolkien's elves entitled the *Songs of the Quendi*? Or are we to believe Freud that there is not such thing as a coincidence? Are Fairy Tales a mythologizing of a people who once were, or are they a genetic message keyed to awaken select individuals at the proper moment (as we were so awakened) so they can evolve into elves? And if the latter is the case, how is this to be done? The answer is, of course, typically elven. It is to be done by magic and enchantment.

214

As we noted earlier, Aleister Crowley (1976) defined magic as the power to make changes at will, while Starhawk used Fortune's/Butler's definition as the power to change consciousness at will, bringing it in accord with Cognitive Psychology. People sometimes ask us if we really believe we are elves. We reply, "We don't believe we are elves. We are elves." While most find this answer mysterious to say the least, it is, in fact, a magical answer. We are not elves because we believe we are elves. We are elves because we live the life elfin. We could believe we were cows, but that wouldn't make us cows. But if we crawled around on all fours and chewed the grass, while we might not appear to be cows physically, we would surely be cows energetically or spiritually. And to the Elven, it is what a person is spiritually/energetically, which is to say what they do and how they live, that truly matters. The material world, we are told by the Buddha is illusion. It is maya. The real world is the world of energy and essence, the world of spirit. The path to Elfin is not outward, as we've said many times previously, but inward. We cannot create Elfin on Earth, nor among the stars, if we don't become elfin within our own lives and actions. The path to Elfin is the path of S'elf Actualization found in the process of Individuation.

The theories (Rogers, 1961) of Carl Råjyrs (spelled in Arvyndase, an elfin language we created that is composed of over 30,000 words. (Silver Elves, 2012g)) are, to the minds of these elves, particularly Aquarian and Elven. The empowerment of the individual, the respect for feelings, the quest to find one's true s'elf and thus happiness are essentially Elfin and Aquarian in nature. Tolkien (1977a) wrote that essential to a true Fairy Tale is the happy or magically miraculous ending. This happiness comes to us by connecting ours'elves to our unconscious and the greater unconscious and thereby empowering the Self as Yung (Jung) conceived it, by the *reinventing of ourselves*, a la Jorj Kële (George Kelly, 1963) and the constant quest to Elf-Actualize.

We sometimes get letters from people who take this all so seriously that they are worried about others who are just "pretending" to be elfin, who are "posers". We always tell these folks to relax, that pretending is the magic of practicing to be. Rolo Mae (May, 1988, p. 50) on writing about Paul Tillich's attraction for women wrote:

"Paulus could also draw women into his life by his extraordinary capacity for fantasy. When I was a senior at the seminary, he gave a lecture one spring afternoon at a college near the city where the young woman lived to whom I was engaged. I had introduced them briefly when she was in New York. She attended the lecture and spoke to Paulus afterward. It being a sunny afternoon, he invited her to go for a walk with him over the campus. They sat down under a tree and he then began a fantasy, inviting her to join him. As was his custom, he wove into it elves, trolls and all sorts of imagined wood sprites, somewhat on the order of Tolkien. The two of them seemed to be living in a primitive land of wood folk, and the theme obviously caught my fiancé's imagination as well as his. At one point, Paulus asked, 'What would we do then?' She – who was not one to suggest such things lightly – answered, 'We would lie together.'"

In fact, we are always more concerned with people who take this all too seriously than those who are pretending. It is simply not Elfin to take ones'elf too seriously and it is definitely elven to play and pretend.

To Carl Råjyrs (Carl Rogers), this drive toward happiness via 'elf-actualization is the primary motivating force of the human species. There we cannot agree. It is one of the two primary drives, as we've indicated in other of our books, the other drive is, as Freud so accurately noted:

The Quest for Immortality

Nearly all stories about Elfin say that we are either immortal or nearly so. This interestingly is also the case of the mythos of the vampire (whom we consider in most cases to be Unseelie or dark elven). The difference is that vampires must drink blood to live, whereas elves have obtained immortality without the need to deprive others of life or blood. The vampire mythos parallels, we believe, humanity's own progress from meat eating, and in some cases cannibalism, to non-killing/vegetarian diet. Although, we should point out that before mankind became meat eaters that they were mostly likely vegetarians, eating fruit and leaves from trees and bushes.

In fact, the story of Cain killing Abel in the Bible from our elven point of view seems to be about the progress from vegetarianism to meat eating. Cain kills Abel because he sacrificed an animal (currently regarded by general society as a demonic act), which was previously forbidden. However, the god of the Bible found the sacrifice pleasing, thus condoned the killing of animals, although He condemned the killing of humans, even when they thems'elves had killed, and put a mark on Cain to signify that he was not to be killed, was under His protection, even though he was exiled. This would seem to be an argument against capital punishment, although it seems few would construe it so.

Currently, the topic most likely to cause the most heated arguments among elves and otherkin in this era concerns vegetarianism vs. meat eating. Yet, these elves believe that we cannot live forever as long as we kill to live. The Vampire existence prolongs life provisionally. To become immortal we must give up killing. This would seem to be in accord with an Aquarian movement toward mutual tolerance. At the same time, we cannot stop people from killing animals; we can only suggest that doing so will lead to a better and healthier life for nearly everyone.

217

Tymlyre (Leary, 1982) prophesied that as we move into space we will also be unlocking the genetic code that controls aging, and we will in due course of time become immortal. But immortality without s'elf actualization merely leads to horror and misery and therefore to a living hell. It is an underlying principle of the Aquarian and Seelie Elven philosophy that we cannot be happy if our happiness is obtained by depriving others. For to be immortal and still kill to live is to infuse the world with misery, a misery that because we caused it is ultimately, in a magical and karmic sense, our own.

As we noted earlier, many of the novels we've cited are about the merging of the normal human and faerie realms. Our move toward immortality is not a one-way endeavor. We are not merely becoming more powerful as physical beings, but we are also becoming in a way, less physical and more ethereal (Freda Warrington's novels, *Elfland*, *Midsummer Night* and *Grail of the Summer Stars* are called the *Aetherial Tales*). Just as our personal myth is made real by uniting it with the "real" world, so too does the living of our myth, spiritualize, etherealize our lives. We are learning through our magic, through our imaginal process, through lucid dreaming and other techniques, to live in those alternate realms of reality, those Quantum Realms of possibility.

The purpose and power of Myth then, as we propose it, is to show us beings who are not mere human beings with all our failings and frailties but with greater or special powers, but rather to show us beings who are more intelligent, more kind, more loving; just a couple of steps beyond us, so that in reaching toward them we become better, greater, more powerful beings ours'elves. For as we become more effective, 'elf actualized beings, we will inevitably create Faerie all about us.

ILLUSTRATIONS

Figure1:
Map of Realm of Nathandyryn,
see page 118.

**Figure 2:
Sun Wheel Talisman, see page 129**

Figure 3:
"Gargy", gargoyle of the Silver Elves,
see page 152

Figure 4:
Love Chant Glyph, see page 157

Figure 5:
Magic Circle, see page 158

*Some individuals try to make fun of the elves
but nearly always fail,
ending up frustrated and angry
while we go merrily on our way,
smiling all the while.
—from the archives of elven history*

ABOUT THE AUTHORS

The Silver Elves, Zardoa and Silver Flame, are a family of elves who have been living and sharing the Elven Way since 1975. They are the authors of 29 books on magic and enchantment, including: *The Book of Elven Runes: A Passage Into Faerie; The Magical Elven Love Letters, volume 1, 2, and 3; An Elfin Book of Spirits: Evoking the Beneficent Powers of Faerie; Caressed by an Elfin Breeze: The Poems of Zardoa Silverstar; Eldafaryn: True Tales of Magic from the Lives of the Silver Elves; Arvyndase (Silverspeech): A Short Course in the Magical Language of the Silver Elves; The Elven Book of Dreams: A Magical Oracle of Faerie; The Book of Elven Magick: The Philosophy and Enchantments of the Seelie Elves, Volume 1 & 2; What An Elf Would Do: A Magical Guide to the Manners and Etiquette of the Faerie Folk; The Elven Tree of Life Eternal: A Magical Quest for One's True S'Elf; Magic Talks: On Being a Correspondence Between the Silver Elves and the Elf Queen's Daughters; Sorcerers' Dialogues: A Further Correspondence Between the Silver Elves and the Founders of the Elf Queen's Daughters; Discourses on High Sorcery: More Correspondence Between the Silver Elves and the Founders of the Elf Queen's Daughters; Ruminations on Necromancy: Continuing Correspondence Between the Silver Elves and the Founders of the Elf Queen's Daughter; The Elven Way: The Magical Path of the Shining Ones; The Book of Elf Names: 5,600 Elven Names to Use for Magic, Game Playing, Inspiration, Naming One's Self and One's Child, and as Words in the Elven Language of the Silver Elves; Elven Silver: The Irreverent Faery Tales of Zardoa Silverstar; An Elven Book of Ryhmes: Book Two of the Magical Poems of Zardoa Silverstar; The Voice of Faerie:*

Making Any Tarot Deck Into an Elven Oracle; Liber Aelph: Words of Guidance from the Silver Elves to our Magical Children; The Shining Ones: The Elfin Spirits That Guide You According to Your Birth Date and the Evolutionary Lessons They Offer: and Elf Magic Mail: Book 1, The Original Letters of the Elf Queen's Daughters with Commentary By The Silver Elves.

The Silver Elves have had various articles published in *Circle Network News Magazine* and have given out over 6,000 elven names to interested individuals in the Arvyndase language, with each elf name having a unique meaning specifically for that person. If you wish to know more about us you can read pages 100 to 107 in *Circles, Groves and Sanctuaries*, compiled by Dan and Pauline Campanelli (Llewellyn Publications, 1992), which contains an article by us and photos us and our home/sanctuary as it existed at the time. We are also mentioned numerous times in *Not In Kansas Anymore* by Christine Wicker (Harper San Francisco, 2005), and *A Field Guide to Otherkin* by Lupa (Megalithica Books, 2007). An interview with the Silver Elves is also included in Emily Carding's recent book *Faery Craft.*

The Elven Way is the spiritual Path of the Elves. It is not a religion. While all elves are free to pursue whatever spiritual path they desire, or not as the case may be, these elves are magicians and follow no particular religious dogma. We do however believe in all the Gods and Goddesses, (also Santa Claus [to whom we're related], the tooth fairy [distant cousins] and the Easter or Ostara Bunny [no relation].) and try to treat them all with due respect. The Elven Way promotes the principles of Fairness, that is to say both Justice, Elegance and Equal Opportunity and Courtesy that is respectful in its interactions and attitude toward all beings, great or small. We understand the world as a magical or miraculous phenomena, and that all beings, by pursuing their own true path, will become whomever they truly desire to be.

Our path is that of Love and Magic and we share our way with all sincerely interested individuals. You can always contact us through our website at: http://silverelves.angelfire.com or join us through our Facebook page, under the name Silver Elves.

The elves say that for most people
the end of the road
is the beginning of the path.
—*Elven Koan*

www.ingramcontent.com/pod-product-compliance
Lightning Source LLC
Chambersburg PA
CBHW060457290526
45791CB00001B/157